Every Family Has One

A Comedy in Three Acts

by George Batson

A Samuel French Acting Edition

SAMUELFRENCH.COM

Copyright © 1942, 1969 by Samuel French, Inc.

ALL RIGHTS RESERVED

CAUTION: Professionals and amateurs are hereby warned that *EVERY FAMILY HAS ONE* is subject to a Licensing Fee. It is fully protected under the copyright laws of the United States of America, the British Commonwealth, including Canada, and all other countries of the Copyright Union. All rights, including professional, amateur, motion picture, recitation, lecturing, public reading, radio broadcasting, television and the rights of translation into foreign languages are strictly reserved. In its present form the play is dedicated to the reading public only.

The amateur live stage performance rights to *EVERY FAMILY HAS ONE* are controlled exclusively by Samuel French, Inc., and licensing arrangements and performance licenses must be secured well in advance of presentation. PLEASE NOTE that amateur Licensing Fees are set upon application in accordance with your producing circumstances. When applying for a licensing quotation and a performance license please give us the number of performances intended, dates of production, your seating capacity and admission fee. Licensing Fees are payable one week before the opening performance of the play to Samuel French, Inc., at 45 W. 25th Street, New York, NY 10010.

Licensing Fee of the required amount must be paid whether the play is presented for charity or gain and whether or not admission is charged.

Stock licensing fees quoted upon application to Samuel French, Inc.

For all other rights than those stipulated above, apply to: Samuel French, Inc.

Particular emphasis is laid on the question of amateur or professional readings, permission and terms for which must be secured in writing from Samuel French, Inc.

Copying from this book in whole or in part is strictly forbidden by law, and the right of performance is not transferable.

Whenever the play is produced the following notice must appear on all programs, printing and advertising for the play: "Produced by special arrangement with Samuel French, Inc."

Due authorship credit must be given on all programs, printing and advertising for the play.

ISBN 978-0-573-60866-7

No one shall commit or authorize any act or omission by which the copyright of, or the right to copyright, this play may be impaired.

No one shall make any changes in this play for the purpose of production.

Publication of this play does not imply availability for performance. Both amateurs and professionals considering a production are strongly advised in their own interests to apply to Samuel French, Inc., for written permission before starting rehearsals, advertising, or booking a theatre.

No part of this book may be reproduced, stored in a retrieval system, or transmitted in any form, by any means, now known or yet to be invented, including mechanical, electronic, photocopying, recording, videotaping, or otherwise, without the prior written permission of the publisher.

MUSIC USE NOTE

Licensees are solely responsible for obtaining formal written permission from copyright owners to use copyrighted music in the performance of this play and are strongly cautioned to do so. If no such permission is obtained by the licensee, then the licensee must use only original music that the licensee owns and controls. Licensees are solely responsible and liable for all music clearances and shall indemnify the copyright owners of the play and their licensing agent, Samuel French, Inc., against any costs, expenses, losses and liabilities arising from the use of music by licensees.

IMPORTANT BILLING AND CREDIT REQUIREMENTS

All producers of *EVERY FAMILY HAS ONE must* give credit to the Author of the Play in all programs distributed in connection with performances of the Play, and in all instances in which the title of the Play appears for the purposes of advertising, publicizing or otherwise exploiting the Play and/or a production. The name of the Author *must* appear on a separate line on which no other name appears, immediately following the title and *must* appear in size of type not less than fifty percent of the size of the title type.

EVERY FAMILY HAS ONE

STORY OF THE PLAY

The Reardons are a typical American family whose eccentricities, if hilarious, are only normal. Laura, the mother, is a social climber who tells tales about her glorious ancestry. She is deliriously happy because she has engineered a match between her daughter, Marcia, and wealthy Sherwin Parker. The youngest Reardon, Penelope, is a demon with a slingshot and the piano. Warry, the only son, is positive he is the coming Eugene O'Neill. Reginald, the father, would rather tinker with the automobile than ticker tape, and Nana, the wise-cracking grandmother, is only concerned with Bing Crosby records and getting rid of the Parkers. Nana succeeds in doing this with the help of Cousin Lily, an adorable liar from down home with stage aspirations. Lily, arriving unexpectedly, agrees to impersonate another Cousin Lily if Nana will help her get an acting job. Her performance as the skeleton in the Reardon closet is so convincing and the lurid facts she reveals so hilariously shocking that the mighty Parkers take to their heels in a hurry and Marcia is reunited with the boy she really loves. Nana returns to her Crosby records with the satisfaction of a job well done and Warry decides that even though his distant relative is a bit on the daft side, she's the only girl for him.

DESCRIPTION OF CHARACTERS

PENELOPE REARDON *is a precocious eleven.*

LAURA REARDON, *the mother of the family, is pretty, young and is fundamentally sound in spite of her often scatterbrained responses.*

MRS. PARKER (BESSIE) *is a tall, aristocratic woman in her late forties. She gives the impression of looking down on everybody and everything.*

NANA REARDON *is an active, vigorous, shrewd lady of sixty-odd years. She has a quick and sharp wit and the habit of saying what she thinks. People call her crotchety until they get to know the generous soul beneath her gruff exterior.*

ESSIE, *the maid of all work, is tall, woebegone, always expects the worst.*

REGINALD REARDON, *the man of the house, is pleasant, easy-going and in his late forties.*

MARCIA REARDON *is sweet, pretty and twenty.*

WARRY *is seventeen. He would be good-looking if he were better groomed.*

MR. PARKER (JAMES) *is big and blustering and fifty.*

SHERWIN PARKER *is twenty-five and good-looking in a plain way.*

LILY REARDON *is a pretty, vibrant girl of seventeen or eighteen.*

TODD GALLOWAY *is tall, good-looking, about twenty-two.*

The following is a copy of program of "EVERY FAMILY HAS ONE" as presented by Northwestern University Theatre, July 29, 30, 31 and August, 1942, in its premiere performances:

EVERY FAMILY HAS ONE

By GEORGE BATSON

THE CHARACTERS
(In the order in which they speak)

PENELOPE REARDON	*Janis Hays*
LAURA REARDON	*Florence Schram*
MRS. JAMES PARKER	*Dixie Fanckboner*
ESSIE	*Katherine Seyl*
NANA REARDON	*Barbara Cattin*
REGINALD REARDON	*Daniel Hauf*
MARCIA REARDON	*Caroline Johnson*
WARRY REARDON	*Charles Morrison*
JAMES PARKER	*James Horne*
SHERWIN PARKER	*Ralph Beeson*
LILY REARDON	*Jo Ann McKeown*
TODD GALLOWAY	*Tom Hayes*

THE SCENES

The action of the play takes place in the living room of the Reardons' home in Fernwood, a suburban town in New Jersey.

ACT ONE—*An afternoon in May—about 4 o'clock.*

Intermission—8 minutes.

ORIGINAL PROGRAM—*Continued*

ACT TWO—*Shortly after dinner that night.*

Intermission—8 minutes.

ACT THREE—*The next morning.*

Clarence A. Miller, Director

Setting designed by Hal Kopel

Every Family Has One

ACT ONE

DESCRIPTION OF SETTING: *The scene is the Reardons' living room in Fernwood, New Jersey, a suburb of New York City. It is a large, bright room of a prosperous, middle-class family, furnished with good taste in a modern adaptation of Georgian Colonial. The wallpaper is a warm yellow in tone, with a large pattern in light blue-green and touches of light magenta, while the woodwork is a warm oyster gray. The room opens off a hallway upstage where, to the Right, is the front door and, to the Left, the door to the dining room and kitchen. A stairway goes up Left to the rooms upstairs. There is a window between the front door and the stair. In the large archway between the room and the hall are two built-in bookshelves, with a fluted column running from each bookshelf to the top of the arch. In the room itself, downstage Right, is a French window opening into a garden. A built-in windowseat is on each side of the French window. Downstage Left is a door into the study. The furniture of the room consists of a sofa with a long table behind it on stage Left Center and an easy chair stage Right Center with a footstool in front of it, a gateleg table to the Left of it, and an ottoman to the Left of the table. In the upstage Right corner of the room is a spinet piano and a bench, and in the up Left corner a radiophonograph and a ladder-back chair. The room contains many dainty touches, such as ivy in glass bowls hanging in the French window, flowers on the bookshelves, etc., that show Laura's decorative instinct. A pleasant, friendly place, it seems especially warm and cheerful this spring afternoon. French doors are partly open, allowing the sunlight to stream in from the garden. The furniture is mostly imitation Colonial with a few authentic pieces for effect. On the sofa are several cushions; behind sofa on the table are a large vase of flowers and several magazines. Telephone on stand in hall up Center. Envelopes piled on table above sofa.*

TIME: *An afternoon in May—about four o'clock.*

As the Curtain rises terrible SOUNDS are in the air. PENELOPE REARDON, *a precocious eleven, is seated at the piano practicing her scales with grim and noisy determination.* PENELOPE *grows tired of playing scales, looks out French door, down Right, then upstairs—all clear, so she starts on "St. Louis Blues." She sings words of chorus, then emits an occasional "Ha-a-a!" in "boogey-woogey" fashion.* PENELOPE *hears* LAURA *singing off up Left on platform, so resumes scales.*

LAURA. *(Enters and stops on platform. She is carrying two vases of flowers)* Penelope, stop that dreadful banging, *please. (Comes down to above* R. *of table* L.C.*)* Mrs. Parker may be resting.

PENELOPE. *(Her hands dropping on her knees)* But Mother, I'm in the mood for music.

LAURA. *(Crosses to above L. end of table—begins arranging flowers after placing them on table)* That racket has nothing to do with music. A mystery why you're forever practicing lately. *(Suspiciously; turns to PENELOPE)* And it seems you only practice when Mrs. Parker is resting.

PENELOPE. I can't help it if she's resting *all* the time.

LAURA. *(Arranging the flowers in the vase)* She does rest a lot, but I guess it's the different climate or something.

PENELOPE. Why?

LAURA. Well, the altitude is higher or maybe it's lower. Anyway, it's different. *(Carries one vase up to bookcase L.)*

PENELOPE. *(Interested)* But why should that make her sleepy?

LAURA. *(Puts down vase)* I don't know *why,* *(Turns to PENELOPE)* Penelope. It just *does.* *(Crosses back to table)* I believe that in New York society women like Mrs. Parker take naps every afternoon.

PENELOPE. *(Sighing)* I wish she'd go back to New York and her society and her *naps.*

LAURA. *(Anxiously. Crosses up to up C. by step, carrying other vase)* Penelope, shh! Suppose Mrs. Parker heard you. She'd be terribly hurt. She might even call off the marriage. And Marcia is very lucky having Sherwin Parker— *(Up to bookcase R.)* one of *the* Parkers—for a fiancé. *(Puts vase on bookcase.)*

PENELOPE. Moms, you know somethin'?

LAURA. Oh, *(Turns to PENELOPE)* that expression! Of course I know something. *(Comes down half step)* What is it?

PENELOPE. *(Telling important news and good joke)* Nana said Sherwin is a codfish.

LAURA. *(In horror)* Nana should be ashamed. Evidently she doesn't appreciate a fine family. *(Crossing to the piano and patting* PENELOPE'S *shoulder)* Won't *you* be proud, dear, when your sister belongs to the four hundred?

PENELOPE. Four hundred what?

LAURA. Four hundred is what we call the society set.

PENELOPE. Why?

LAURA. I don't know why, Penelope. We just *do*.

PENELOPE. *(Thoughtfully, finger to forehead)* Well, if Marcia belongs will she have to take a nap every afternoon?

(MRS. PARKER *begins to come downstairs.*)

LAURA. *(Wearily)* Penelope, go outside and play. *(Crosses down* R.; *opens French door)* You're giving mother a headache. *(Crosses* L. *to down Center.* MRS. PARKER (BESSIE) *enters from* R. *A tall, aristocratic woman in her late forties, she gives the impression of looking down on everybody and everything.* LAURA *sees her; crosses to her)* Oh, Mrs. Parker, did we wake you?

MRS. PARKER. *(Going to the sofa)* No, I had set the alarm. (LAURA *motions* MRS. PARKER *to a seat on center of sofa.* MRS. PARKER *sits. As* PENELOPE *resumes her scales)* My, is she *never* away from that piano?

LAURA. *(Down to* MRS. PARKER. LAURA *turns toward* PENELOPE*)* I was the same way when I was a child. *(Half step toward* PENELOPE*)* Penelope, not now! *(Two more steps toward her)* Go play with lovely little *(Gesture)* whosis who moved next door yesterday. *(Turns back toward* MRS. PARKER.*)*

PENELOPE. *(Picks up slingshot from piano bench)*

Her name isn't whosis. *(Crosses down to French doors; begins playing with slingshot as she goes)* It's Maudie.

LAURA. Well, *(Turns toward* PENELOPE*)* play with her anyway. *(Reaction as she sees slingshot. By this time* PENELOPE *is down to French doors. Steps toward her)* And leave that slingshot here. (PENELOPE *turns toward* L.) I'm sure Maudie hasn't a slingshot.

PENELOPE. Maybe not *(Regretfully tossing the slingshot into the easy chair)* but she's got a peachy air rifle and lots of buckshot. *(Turns and skips out through French door.)*

LAURA. *(Reaction, then turns to* MRS. PARKER *with helpless gesture)* Children, they're so—so childish. *(Crosses to sofa, above* MRS. PARKER*)* Our new neighbors look lovely. *(Sits)* Anyway, I saw fine furniture going in. There's a rumor that they're related to *the* Winthrops. They signed the Declaration of Independence. Or was it the Emancipation Proclamation?

MRS. PARKER. The Plymouth Charter, I think.

LAURA. Well, something historical, anyway.

MRS. PARKER. *(Gushingly)* It's been *too* sweet of you to have me here while Mr. Parker and Sherwin were away. My little apartment in New York would have been so lonely without them. Twenty rooms, you know, *are* lonely when they're *empty*—in spite of all the servants. And then, too, this has given us the chance to become acquainted. You're such a remarkable family. Never a harsh word, never a quarrel—

LAURA. Oh, we get along famously. Of course, I have to make concessions, but then that's why mothers are born.

(There is the sudden sound of someone TYPING furiously on an old and noisy typewriter. Both

WOMEN *look toward the study. TYPING continues softly.)*

MRS. PARKER. What's he writing now?
LAURA. *(Rises; crosses to study door)* Another book. (MRS. PARKER *moves L. on sofa and turns, facing study)* He just finishes one and goes right ahead with another. *(Closes door.)*
MRS. PARKER. *(As the noise of typing continues, but not so loudly)* He certainly *sounds* energetic. (LAURA *turns toward* MRS. PARKER) Does he just sit in there, writing all the time?
LAURA. *(Crossing toward* MRS. PARKER*)* Well, every now and then he gets up and *paces. (Sits L. of* MRS. PARKER.*)*
MRS. PARKER. You know Mr. Parker is still willing to give him that job.
LAURA. Just wait until he discovers his first book isn't the masterpiece he thinks it is. Why, none of the Reardons were writers. *(Airily)* No, they were all just adventurers. I *did* tell you that one of my ancestors was with Sir Walter Raleigh when he discovered the Fountain of Youth?
MRS. PARKER. It's such a comfort, tracing your family way back. And not being afraid of what you'll find. That's one thing Mr. Parker and I demanded, that our Sherwin marry into a family as fine as our own. *(TYPING makes a last spurt—then stops. After typing stops)* Couldn't he get a noiseless?
LAURA. He's—he's sentimental. *(With a sigh)* I do worry. He's not going through this stage as fast as he went through the others. You know, the fireman stage, the baseball player stage. Once he even wanted to go to the Klondike and yell *(Dramatise— arm up in air)* "mush—mush" at a lot of dogs.
MRS. PARKER. Often I've looked up and caught him staring at me *so* strangely. *(Mimic stare, using*

glasses) Such an expression. Oh, well, perhaps he was studying *(Smoothing down corset)* my character.

LAURA. Yes, he does write about practically *anything*. *(Hand to face)* Oh, dear, I mean— *(Quickly, reaching out and touching arm of* MRS. PARKER *reassuringly)* If I make him give up writing he'll blame me all his life. I just can't have that. There's nothing worse than wanting to do something and not get the chance to do it. *(Softly)* I—I always wanted to sing, but my parents wouldn't let me study it. I've always had regrets. That's why I want Warry to find out for himself.

MRS. PARKER. But remember *(CLOCK strikes five)* spare the rod and— *(Glancing at her watch. Rises on line)* Heavens, the train is due any moment. *(Crosses to up* C.*)* I'd better hurry if I'm to meet Sherwin and his father.

LAURA. *(Rises.* MRS. PARKER *turns toward* L.*)* Don't you want me to drive down with you? *(Up to* MRS. PARKER.*)*

MRS. PARKER. *(As they start up to arch)* No, thank you. I'll find the station easily enough.

LAURA. *(As they go off up through arch to* R.*)* Do hurry—for Marcia's sake. She hasn't seen Sherwin for three weeks. And when you're in love three weeks is just three eternities. *(Last part of line is from offstage. The stage is deserted for a second.)*

(NANA REARDON *enters through the French doors. An active, vigorous, shrewd lady of sixty-odd years,* NANA *has a quick and sharp wit and the habit of saying what she thinks. People call her crotchety until they get to know the generous soul beneath her gruff exterior. She dresses simply.* NANA *carries in box of chocolate mints and a record album of latest Bing Crosby cowboy songs—puts records and candy on table down*

R.C., then starts taking off light-weight coat as ESSIE *enters from dining room through center arch.* ESSIE, *the maid of all work, steps down both steps from level to floor in one step.* ESSIE *is tall, woebegone; always expects the worst. She is carrying a small tray with a glass of milk and several doughnuts on it.)*

NANA. *(Turns as she hears* ESSIE *enter)* Where are you going, my pretty maid?

ESSIE. *(Turns back to* NANA*)* Just taking some doughnuts in to Mr. Warry. (NANA *puts coat on chair)* If you ask me, he must be hungry, banging away in there all day. Of course, nobody asked me—

NANA. No wonder the boy is never hungry at mealtime. Well, go ahead, fill him up. Here— *(Crosses to* ESSIE *and takes two doughnuts)* Let me taste one. *(Tasting one)* Umm—good. (ESSIE *crosses down* L. *to door to study)* Not so light as the kind I made. But they're good, Essie.

ESSIE. *(At the study door, unhappily. Turns to* NANA*)* I know they're good. They're for the Parkers. I don't know what this house is coming to. Doughnuts for breakfast. *(With foreboding)* And tonight at dinner I'm to serve finger-bowls.

NANA. What—to eat?

ESSIE. No, to dip your fingers in. And I'm to put napkins on just the same. *(She shakes her head and goes into the study.)*

(NANA *smiles after her and crosses down to below table down* R.C., *eating the doughnut as* REGINALD REARDON *enters* C. *from* L. *carrying tools.* REGINALD, *the man of the house, is pleasant, easy-going and in his late forties. He is dressed in overalls and carries a hammer, a saw and a small kit of tools. He is singing "Heigh ho! Heigh ho! It's off to work we go" as he enters.)*

ACT I   EVERY FAMILY HAS ONE   17

REGINALD. *(Sees doughnut held in* NANA'S *hand as he approaches her. He puts tools down on ottoman and kit on floor—takes doughnut, bites into it)* Yum, what doughnuts! Nothing like doughnuts after a hard day's work.

NANA. *(Drily)* I thought that was why you didn't go into the office today. You needed a rest.

REGINALD. *(Cheerfully)* I know, Mother—but all these little things around here needed fixing, so I thought—

NANA. I know what you thought. Can't fool me, my son. You're never happy unless you're all dressed up like a wrecking crew, putting something out of commission. *(Crosses to chair; picks up coat and slingshot.)*

REGINALD. You won't call me a wrecking crew when you see how I'm going to fix the car.

NANA. I remember that last time you fixed the car. *(Sits chair* R.C., *holding her coat in her lap; puts slingshot on table)* The bottom fell out.

REGINALD. Now, now, Mother—that's a slight exaggeration. It was only the motor that fell out. *(Finishing the doughnut)* Just like you used to make. Why don't you ever do any more baking, Mother?

NANA. Because according to Laura, a lady mustn't be seen in the kitchen in these parts. It just isn't done. *(Soberly)* Laura worries me, Reginald. What's gotten into her since Marcia met that Sherwin Parker? She just isn't herself.

REGINALD. Oh, you know how it is. The Parkers are mighty important society folks and Laura's trying to impress them.

NANA. Pooh! Pooh! There's something trickey about those Parkers. People who *really* are important don't go around talking about it all the time. Anyway, he's too anxious to get you to merge your business with his.

REGINALD. *(Quickly picks up tools and kit)* He just thinks it would be profitable for both of us. *(Crosses to the French door)* You're prejudiced.

NANA. I'm (REGINALD *stops and turns back to* NANA*)* also sure he knows about your being promised that Government contract. Do you think Laura told Mrs. Parker about it?

REGINALD. Laura talks a lot but she never tells secrets. Don't tell her I'm out in the driveway. *(He throws this line over his shoulder as he exits)* She never wants me to be seen in public in overalls.

NANA. *(Calling after him as he exits.* ESSIE *begins backing out of study, acting as if she had seen an apparition)* Be sure and put the brakes on this time. Oh, Essie, (ESSIE *turns with a start when* NANA *speaks to her)* will you hang my coat up, please?

ESSIE. *(Crossing to take coat—reaches for it with trembling hand)* Sure, ma'm.

NANA. *(Looking at her)* You look sort of pale.

ESSIE. *(Nervously)* Mr. Warry just read me the first chapter of his new book. If you ask me, this younger generation is something frightening. Of course, nobody asked me— *(Starts out up* C. NANA *picks up magazine from table and starts to look at it.)*

LAURA. *(Entering from* R. *in arch. As* LAURA *comes down off steps)* Oh, here you are, Essie. You can start the dinner. The Parkers will all be here any minute now.

ESSIE. Yes'm. *(Turns and starts out.)*

LAURA. *(Correctingly)* Yes, *Mrs. Reardon.* (*This stops* ESSIE, *who turns back toward* L.*)*

ESSIE. Yes'm, Mrs. Reardon. *(Exits off up* L. LAURA *reacts up* C.*)*

LAURA. *(As* ESSIE *goes—turns to* NANA*)* Nana, I don't know what to do about Essie. She simply has no *chic*. It's impossible to entertain with her here.

NANA. *(Smilingly)* She's been entertaining *me* for the past ten years.

LANRA. *(Crosses down to ottoman R.C.)* I know, but *now*—now that our Marcia is marrying into the *(Sits)* cream of New York society.

NANA. We're all just people.

LAURA. Perhaps, but there are people *and* people.

NANA. Well, I'm glad the Parkers aren't *my* people. *(Shuddering)* Been bad enough having her here the past two weeks. Now we're going to have them all for the week-end. I wish they'd go home so we could be ourselves again.

LAURA. Why, how ridiculous! We have been ourselves.

NANA. Laura Clark, I knew you when you were a little girl back in St. Peter's and Reginald used to carry your books home from school. I've known you almost as long as you've known yourself, but I've never seen you act as daffy as you have since you met these Parkers.

LAURA. *(Proudly. Up)* I've made a wonderful match for my daughter and nothing is going to ruin my plans. *(Crosses to up L.C.)* Oh, what's the use? I try to elevate my family but they just won't be elevated. *(Turns to* NANA*)* We should have stayed in St. Peter's and never moved here. *(Business of fixing hair and* NANA *reacts disgust and foot tapping)* But I wanted my babies to meet the right people.

NANA. What was wrong with the folks back in St. Peter's?

LAURA. *(Stiffly)* After all, Nana, Marcia could never have met a boy like Sherwin Parker in that little fishing village.

NANA. *(Grimly)* Don't I know it?

LAURA. *(At the sound of loud HAMMERING from the driveway)* Gracious, what's that knocking?

(HAMMERING momentarily stops.)

NANA. *(Simply)* Essie—shelling peas.

(Terrific BANGING, then continues lightly.)

LAURA. It sounds like— Can it be? Oh, can it be—? *(With growing suspicion as she marches toward the French doors)* If that's Reginald being mechanical—in *public*—I'll just scream. *(Opening screen and looking out—holds screen door open. Just inside the doorway)* It *is* Reginald— *(Calling sternly)* Reginald, you come in here this very minute. *(HAMMERING stops. Suddenly sweet as she spies her new neighbor across the driveway)* Oh, hello, Mrs. Winthrop— Yes, just a lovely day— How do you like it here in Fernwood? Oh, I couldn't think of living anywhere else— Oh— It's so—so select. *(Affectionately)* That's all right, Reginald darling. I just wondered where you were. *(Resume HAMMERING. Turning back to* NANA*)* Of all the disgraceful exhibitions! *(Lets screen door slam)* Out there under the car—in *overalls*.

NANA. What do you expect him to wear under the car— *(Leans toward* LAURA*)* a tuxedo?

LAURA. *(Going to extra chair against wall up* L.*)* Sometimes I feel like giving up. I try so hard and for what? *(Surveying the piles of envelopes as she moves chair to above table)* Oh, these invitations! I still haven't sent out half of them. I should have hired a social secretary. Mrs. Parker said she didn't know how I got along without one. *(Sits.)*

NANA. *(Getting record album)* Did you send any to our relatives back in the old home town?

LAURA. A few. St. Peter's is so far away none of them would come—thank goodness.

NANA. *(Angrily)* There is nothing wrong with our relatives.

LAURA. Just the same, I shouldn't want the Parkers to meet them. They're simple and poor. I told the Parkers they were aristocrats and millionaires.

NANA. *(Up, holding record album)* Then I wish some of them would come to the wedding. *(Begins to cross to phonograph)* It would serve you right.

LAURA. Oh, they won't! I sent an invitation to poor Lily. (NANA *stops up* C. *and exclaims: "Lily?"*) I thought it would make her feel good. All of us have been unkind to her. After all, it was none of our business whom she married—as long as she keeps him up there.

NANA. Lily, our third cousin. Will you ever forget when she was thirteen and ran away with the circus? She wanted to be a bareback rider but she frightened all the horses.

LAURA. And when she was fourteen she stowed away on a boat bound for Brazil because she liked Brazil nuts.

NANA. Oh, well, *(Crossing to radio-phonograph)* she only got as far as Boston.

LAURA. *(Reflectively)* She was certainly full of girlish pranks—and things. (NANA *puts down album.* LAURA, *sadly)* But why did she marry that man? She knew he was engaged in an—illegal enterprise.

NANA. Come out and say it. *(Step toward* R.*)* He was a bootlegger.

LUARA. *(In horror)* Nana, ssh! Suppose the children heard you.

NANA. He wasn't the only bootlegger in St. Peter's.

LAURA. He was the only one who got caught.

NANA. *(Teasingly. Crosses behind* LAURA *and stops* R. *of her)* You know, you never can tell about Lily. She might get that invitation and come.

LAURA. All the way from St. Peter's when we haven't seen her in twenty years? Never. (NANA *over to bookcase up* R.C. *Addressing envelopes)* After all, every family has a *skeleton*.

NANA. *(Gets workbasket off shelf and turns to* L.*)* Lily was no *skeleton*. The last time I saw her she was running a candy store and eating all the profits. She weighed a good two hundred.

LAURA. *(Looking up)* Oh, I'm sure she won't come. What a terrible thought! Lily *here*. *(Hopefully)* Perhaps she won't even get the invitation. I didn't know her husband's name, so I just addressed it to Miss Lily Reardon. *(Chewing the end of her pen)* Just to make sure, I'm going to go ask that fortune-teller in Newark. *(More HAMMERING can be heard from the driveway. On sound of hammering* NANA *comes down and looks out French doors)* What *is* Reginald doing?

NANA. *(Turns toward* L.*)* He calls it *fixing* the car.

LAURA. I wish he had some quiet hobby like stamps or guppies. *(As* REGINALD *ceases his hammering on the car the TYPING is resumed in the study.* LAURA *puts her hands to her head, throwing her pen down in despair)* And now *he* starts the Anvil Chorus.

(MARCIA *begins coming downstairs.)*

NANA. *(Looking toward the study. Crossing to chair* R.C.*)* Wonder what this new book is about. *(Sits.)*

LAURA. I couldn't even understand that first one. It frightened me.

NANA. Maybe he's a genius.

LAURA. *(Positively)* It wasn't *that* frightening.

(MARCIA REARDON *enters the room from upstairs. Sweet, pretty and twenty,* MARCIA *is wearing her wedding dress, a simple and attractive gown.* MARCIA *also wearing her veil—simple, thrown back.)*

MARCIA. *(As she finishes coming downstairs. Standing up* C. *on steps)* Well, here's the finished product. Like it, Mother? Mrs. Daley says it's her greatest creation.
LAURA. *(Rising excitedly and going up* L.C.*)* Darling, how simply too beautiful!
MARCIA. *(Going to above the easy chair)* Your opinion, Nana?
NANA. *(Proudly)* You look almost as lovely as I did.
MARCIA. Then *(Kissing the top of her head)* I look pretty gosh-darned lovely!
LAURA. Turn around, dear. (MARCIA *comes around* NANA's *chair to down* R. *and rotates)* My baby! I'm beginning to realize I'm losing my little girl. *(Tearfully)* If I had time I'd just sit down and cry.
MARCIA. Don't forget you still have Warry and Penelope.
LAURA. *(Standing* L.C. *by sofa)* Oh, wait until Sherwin sees you. But he mustn't. It's bad luck or something. Not that we could have any bad luck, not that we could have bad luck at all, but *do* take it off before he gets here.
ESSIE. *(Standing in the arch up* C., *holding large cooking spoon)* Pardon, ma'm. I mean, Mrs. Reardon. But I had two dozen doughnuts for breakfast tomorrow. Now I only got six.
LAURA. *(Puzzled)* Six?
ESSIE. I had them in the window cooling off. I had to go into my room and when I came back they were gone.
LAURA. *(Crossing up to* ESSIE*)* Why, someone must have taken them.

ESSIE. *(Drily)* If you ask me they'd be the first doughnuts I ever cooked that could *walk*.

LAURA. Penelope, of course.

ESSIE. Don't see how Penelope could eat—er—er— How many would that be? *(Tries mental arithmetic but gives up)* Six from two dozen, that leaves— Well, I don't see how little Penelope could eat all those doughnuts.

LAURA. Never mind, Essie. We shall have crepe suzettes for breakfast. *(Turns and starts to come down L.C.)*

ESSIE. *(Starts out up L.)* Crepe— *(Stops and turns in horror)* crepe what?!

LAURA. *(Turns up to ESSIE)* Pancakes, Essie—pancakes.

ESSIE. *(Relieved)* Oh, that's more like it. *(She exits.)*

LAURA. *(Crossing to down C.)* Marcia, is Mrs. Daley still upstairs?

MARCIA. *(Crossing to LAURA)* Yes, she wants to know if you like the dress.

LAURA. It's beautiful. *(Crosses MARCIA and goes up steps. MARCIA crosses L.)* And I'll go right up and congratulate her— *(In arch up C. Turns back)* My little girl—my *baby*—a bride. *(She sighs and exits.)*

NANA. *(Watching MARCIA as she starts removing veil and puts it on table L.C.)* Happy?

MARCIA. *(Sitting on the arm of the sofa)* Of course.

NANA. Don't act it. *(Sharply)* Do you really love this—this son-of-a-Plymouth-Rock?

MARCIA. *(Sharply almost)* I'd hardly marry him if I didn't.

NANA. Maybe it's the trend of the times, but when I was marrying your grandfather I was excited and happy and thrilled. And so proud I told the world.

MARCIA. *(Quietly, with gesture)* Ah, but we moderns don't show our emotions. We hide them.

NANA. Times have changed but love hasn't.

MARCIA. *(Nervously)* Shall I turn a few handsprings and giggle and blush?

NANA. No giggles, I warn you. But you could be a trifle gaga.

MARCIA. Don't worry about me. *(Rises)* Sherwin is a grand catch. Mother is crazy about him.

NANA. She's not marrying him. *You* are.

MARCIA. *(Step toward* NANA*)* He comes from a fine family.

NANA. *(Disgustedly)* Family again. The only prominent American they haven't claimed is Pocahontas. And they'll be saying her name was Pocahontas Parker before long.

REGINALD. *(Enters through the French doors, his face heavily streaked with grease)* Well, well, if it isn't my little girl!

MARCIA. *(As he stops, admiring her. Pointing in feigned horror)* Heavens, are you my father?

REGINALD. *(Admiringly)* And proud to be. *(He crosses to take her in his arms and she backs away)* You look like a million.

MARCIA. Just *look*, Dad—don't touch.

REGINALD. *(Turns to* NANA*)* Proud of your grandchild, Nana?

NANA. Certainly. Anyone can see whom she resembles.

REGINALD. *(Proudly patting abdomen and putting arms out)* Sure, she's the image of her old man.

NANA. With your face all streaked you look more like Topsy's old man.

REGINALD. *(With a loud sigh)* It seems I'm only getting to know Marcia when I'm losing her.

NANA. *(Acidly)* Ah, you're not losing your daughter. You're gaining a son.

REGINALD. *(Steps toward* NANA*)* Splendid chap, Sherwin. Going to go places, too.

NANA. I'd like to tell you where. *(Shaking her head)* I don't like prunes on the menu—less in the family.

MARCIA. He's the best to come along. *(Goes around downstage end of sofa and up to above table.)*

NANA. What about—Todd Galloway?

REGINALD. *(Quickly. Crosses to above* NANA's *chair with hushing gesture)* Now, Mother, why bring him up? Marcia hasn't thought of him for months.

NANA. *(Unconvinced)* Oh, no?

MARCIA. *(Looking at the envelopes, but her voice betrays her feelings)* Fine husband material, that Todd Galloway. Reckless, irresponsible, selfish—

NANA. Reminds me of your grandfather. Can never be certain of him, but oh, how you do wish you could.

MARCIA. *(Drops envelopes and crosses down L. to end of sofa, with back to* NANA *and* REGINALD*)* He went away without saying goodbye. He never even wrote to me. Well, I'll show that Todd Galloway a thing or two!

REGINALD. *(Going toward her, comfortingly.* MARCIA *turns as* REGINALD *crosses)* Now, Marcia, don't think about him, Marcia. Nana shouldn't have mentioned him. *(Walking to the arch up* C.*)* Well, I've got to get a screwdriver. See you later. *(He exits* L.*)*

MARCIA. Why— *(Crosses above table)* why did you mention Todd?

NANA. Warry saw him downtown this morning.

MARCIA. *(Crossing down to ottoman)* Did—did Warry mention how he looked?

NANA. I guess Todd has managed to stay in one piece.

MARCIA. I thought he'd gone away for good.
NANA. Perhaps he has come home for *good*.

(MARCIA *is about to speak when* LAURA *re-enters from upstairs.)*

LAURA. *(Entering and coming down to above sofa)* Oh, darling, please change before Sherwin gets here. (MARCIA *starts up toward up* C.) Mrs. Daley is going to mail these invitations for me. (MARCIA *crosses to table for wedding veil as* LAURA *puts chair against back wall.)*
WARRY. *(Calling from the study)* Oh, say, Mother!
LAURA. *(Turns and steps toward study)* What is it, Warry?
WARRY. Which is a *household* word— (MARCIA *starts to cross up* C. *toward arch)* decapitate or assassinate?
LAURA. *(Angrily. Crosses down to study door) Neither* is a household word. (REGINALD *enters up* C. *from* L., *carrying screwdriver. Shuddering. Turns back toward* NANA) Another *horrible* book. *(Sees* REGINALD; *gasps)* Who are *you?*
REGINALD. *(Happily coming down* C.) I'm your husband—remember?
LAURA. *(Crossly)* Haven't I enough to worry about without you putting on a minstrel show?
REGINALD. *(Crossing to French doors)* I'll be finished out here in a minute.
LAURA. *(Steps toward* REGINALD *as he stops)* But the Parkers are arriving.
REGINALD. Laura, *(Turns toward* LAURA*)* the car will never bother us again.
LAURA. Will it ever *go* again?
REGINALD. Now, Mother, you know what I did to the sink.
NANA. No one in town will ever forget.

LAURA. *(Remembering. Crosses to* L. *of table by ottoman)* Oh, and Reginald, be sure you shave before dinner.

REGINALD. *(Protesting)* But this is my day of rest. I shaved yesterday.

LAURA. No matter. Mr. Parker shaves twice every day.

NANA. *(Thinking aloud)* I hope his razor slips.

(REGINALD *exits French doors and TYPING starts quietly.)*

LAURA. *(Crosses up to steps; turns)* Nana, you *are* dressing for dinner? *(Exits upstairs.)*

NANA. *(Rising and crossing to* C., *then up)* I'm putting on my comfortable shoes if that's what you mean. *(Turns)* If the Parkers don't like my dress they can eat in the kitchen. *(She follows* LAURA *out. Exits upstairs.)*

MARCIA. Warry, oh, Warry! *(TYPING stops)* You haven't seen my wedding dress.

WARRY. *(From the study)* Be right out. Just let me finish this sentence. (MARCIA *puts veil on as she comes down* C. WARRY *TYPES about a line.)*

(WARRY *comes out of the study. He is seventeen, dressed in a sweater and grey trousers. He would be good-looking if he were better groomed. He has an eyeshade pushed up on his hair. Crosses to below end of sofa. Whistles appreciatively. Begins cross to inspect her.)*

MARCIA. *(Posing for his inspection. As she turns and* WARRY *walks around her)* Well, Mr. Shakespeare?

WARRY. Golly, Sis, you look great!

MARCIA. *(As she curtsies)* Thank you, sir! Tell me, how's the new epic?

WARRY. *(Seriously)* Oh, all right. But heck, I

can't do it full justice. There's too much excitement around here. Too much noise. *(Holding hand on forehead)* I can't really concentrate.

MARCIA. It will be quiet enough after the wedding.

WARRY. Oh, yeah? *(Crossing to down R.C., dramatizing)* I'll have Penelope *(Piano-playing gesture)* and her piano and Mom and her bridge parties *(Gesture)* and Nana and her Bing Crosby records. *(Leaning against table and turning toward* MARCIA*)* No, Marcia, this atmosphere—well, it just isn't conducive for creating.

MARCIA. *(Amused and starting to remove veil)* I hear you can buy lovely mountain tops out West dirt cheap.

WARRY. *(Straightens up; snaps fingers)* Say! Not a bad idea, Marcia. I'll look into it. *(Steps R., thinking.)*

MARCIA. Before you buy Pike's Peak, young man, wait until you get your first check.

WARRY. *(Crossing, taking off eyeshade.* MARCIA *moves R.)* Oh, I'll get it soon. The publishers have had my first book two weeks. *(Throws eyeshade on table)* I guess they're giving it careful consideration, but I wish they'd hurry up.

MARCIA. *(Preparing him)* But you're so young, Warry—and you've had no experience.

WARRY. *(Turns. Stoutly)* I've had experience. *(Step and half toward her)* You can't call anyone who's gone through all that I have *inexperienced.

MARCIA. What are all these things you've gone through?

WARRY. Well, *(Sinks back to arm of sofa)* I had a brace on my teeth *(Sits on arm)* and high school, for example—and—

MARCIA. Good luck, anyway, Warry.

WARRY. Not that I'll win prizes right off—but eventually—

MARCIA. *(Putting veil down and picking up maga-*

zine from table R.C. *With much feigned pride)* And to think I'm *your* sister. *(Sits on ottoman. Casually)* Been writing all day?

WARRY. *(Sinks back on sofa, legs over end; reaches over head for pillow; puts pillow under his head)* Went downtown once. To get some carbon paper.

MARCIA. Anything exciting happen?

WARRY. No—just got the carbon paper.

MARCIA. *(Relentlessly)* Meet anyone?

WARRY. Ran into Minnie Tuttle.

MARCIA. Oh, *(Slams magazine down in lap)* hang Minnie Tuttle! *(Regains previous attempt at outward calm)* I mean, she's not very exciting.

WARRY. *(Swinging left leg down onto floor and raising head slightly)* Oh, yes, Todd Galloway. I ran into him, too.

MARCIA. *(Lightly and starting to look at magazine again)* Oh, is he back in town?

WARRY. Guess he must be if I met him.

MARCIA. How did he look?

WARRY. Same old Todd.

MARCIA. Did—did you talk to him?

WARRY. A bit. He asked for you. *(Swings right foot to floor and sits up)* Say, guess what?

MARCIA. *(Throws magazine on table, rises and crosses to* WARRY; *excitedly)* What?

WARRY. *(Stands)* I've got the most terrific ending for the book. Instead of them all committing suicide I'm going to have a couple of them guillotined. *(Hand cut off head from back)* Then the hero and the heroine can *(Exaggerated swimming motions as he crosses* R.C.*)* swim through the sharks and—

MARCIA. *(Crosses to below sofa and turns)* Sounds too cozy. (WARRY *turns)* I mean, how thrilling.

WARRY. *(Teasing—hands on hips. Wisely)* You mean, did *he* ask about you.

ACT I   EVERY FAMILY HAS ONE   31

MARCIA. He? What *he?* What are you talking about?

WARRY. *(Knowingly, with hand)* That's all right. I know you're crazy about him.

MARCIA. *(Sits downstage end of sofa)* I don't know what you're talking about. *(Smoothing hair and turning away.)*

WARRY. *(Crosses to upstage end of sofa. Smiling infuriatingly)* Sister mine, you do everything but carry a sandwich board *(Kneeling and dramatizing)* with *I love Todd* written on it in big red letters.

MARCIA. *(Turning back to him)* You're being so silly. Your love of the dramatic has you on the wrong track this time. *(Turns head away again.)*

WARRY. *(Up)* You should just *(Leaning across end of sofa, head in left hand)* see yourself, Miss Lonelyhearts, when you were asking all these questions about him.

MARCIA. *(Facing him)* And I suppose Todd loves me, too?

WARRY. *(Straightening up. With conviction)* Sure he does.

MARCIA. He went away four months ago. Never even said goodbye.

WARRY. There could be a reason.

MARCIA. *(To front)* I can't think of any.

WARRY. Marrying one guy and loving another. *(Going to her)* Marcia, what's the matter with you?

MARCIA. Mother would never forgive me if I didn't marry Sherwin.

WARRY. *(Crossing C. In despair)* Women. I can't figure them out. *(Turns. Quickly)* At least, I can't figure *all* of them out.

MARCIA. If it will help you any, I *did* love Todd. At least, I was fond of him when we both were in high school. He's good-looking and romantic and he dances well but— Oh, those things aren't important.

WARRY. *(Crosses to sofa)* Hope you can tell yourself that when you're Mrs. Sherwin Parker and not *(Sits on arm)* kick the *(Gesture up)* roof off the house.

MARCIA. *(Rises)* Oh—oh, *(Crosses to table* R.C.*; gets veil; starts out up* C.*)* let's not discuss it any more. Todd is completely out of my life.

WARRY. *(Maddeningly)* Says you. *(Picks up sofa pillow and hugs it.)*

MARCIA. *(Stops and turns. Angrily)* I tell you he is.

WARRY. *(Shrugging his shoulders)* Maybe.

(MARCIA *starts to go up onto steps; heads for stairs —stopped by* LAURA's *entrance.)*

LAURA. *(Entering from upstairs)* Marcia, dear, *please* get dressed for dinner. (MARCIA *exits upstairs as* LAURA *comes down* C.*)* And, Warry, you're not going to sit at the table like that. Why do you insist upon wearing that horrible sweater?

WARRY. *You* knitted it.

LAURA. *(Crosses. Hurt)* I could hardly expect any appreciation from you. The way I simply slaved over that. And it's real Angora, too. *(Angora business—plucks fuzz.* WARRY *reacts. Angrily)* Stop grinning, Warry Reardon, and change your clothes. *(Pushing his hair back)* And do something about that mop of hair, too.

WARRY. Well, I could bleach it.

NANA. *(Enters from upstairs. She has changed to her comfortable shoes)* Here's Cousin Jessie's address, Laura. *(She hands* LAURA *a slip of paper.)*

LAURA. *(Going above table* L.C. *with it)* Thanks, Nana. Her husband is in the jewelry business. We *must* send them an invitation.

NANA. *(Going to the easy chair)* His last name is MacTavish. *(Sits)* They'll send a salt spoon.

LAURA. Well, we can hope, can't we? Now, Warry, go dress.

WARRY. *(Up, giving pillow a throw over head to floor front of sofa)* The Parkers are coming—hurray—hurray—hurray!

NANA. Oh— Pooh!

LAURA. Charming expression for a lady of culture.

NANA. Even Emily Post would forget her culture around the Parkers.

LAURA. *(Crossing to pick up pillow)* But, Nana, you're encouraging the children to be disrespectful toward them. Penelope called Sherwin a—a codfish. *(Bends to pick up pillow.)*

NANA. A masterpiece of understatement.

PENELOPE. *(She comes skipping in through the French doors)* Hy, folks!

LAURA. Oh, *(Straightening up with pillow)* Penelope, (PENELOPE *stopping in her tracks at* C.) I want to ask you about something.

PENELOPE. *(Turns)* Whatever it is I didn't break it.

LAURA. Nothing's broken—I hope. *(Puts pillow on sofa and crosses up to* PENELOPE.)

PENELOPE. Whew! *(Gesture of relief.)*

LAURA. It's about some doughnuts.

PENELOPE. *(Quickly)* I didn't take any doughnuts.

LAURA. *(Wisely)* Ah, but did you tell Maudie where they were and ask her to take them?

PENELOPE. *(With disgust)* I wouldn't give her a doughnut if she hadn't eaten for a week.

LAURA. Penelope, don't talk that way.

PENELOPE. I don't like Maudie. *(With gesture of distaste)* She's—she's odious. *(Sits with a bang on the couch. Punctuates each beat with bounce)* And-I-didn't-take-any-doughnuts. *(Bounce several times.)*

LAURA. Stop bouncing on that sofa. You'll break the springs.

PENELOPE. *(Bouncing to downstage end of sofa. Assuredly)* Pops-will-love-to-fix-'em.

LAURA. *(Sternly)* Because of this you'll not go to the movies on Saturday.

PENELOPE. *(Jumping up in anguish)* But it's chapter eighteen of the serial. *(Hands over head, standing on tiptoes as if holding on)* Last week Beulah Love was hanging from the cliff and the villain *(Jumping up and down)* was dancing on her manicure.

LAURA. *(Staring in horror at* PENELOPE'S *feet as she continues jumping)* That's no sight for any child to see.

PENELOPE. *(Sitting on leg on downstage end of sofa. Pleadingly)* But, Moms, they're giving out comic books, too.

LAURA. Those doughnuts never walked away.

PENELOPE. Someone else might have stolen them. Some tramp or something.

REGINALD. *(Enters hurriedly through the French doors;* LAURA *turns as* REGINALD *speaks)* Say, Laura, have we any bicarbonate in the house?

LAURA. Yes, there's some in the medicine chest. Don't you feel well?

REGINALD. I feel sort of— Oh, I feel *terrible. (He groans and exits up* L., LAURA *following to up* C., *puzzled.)*

NANA. *(Looking after him)* Something he ate, no doubt.

LAURA. *(Comprehending)* Oh, I see. *(Turning back to* PENELOPE*)* Very well, Penelope, dear. *(Crosses down to sofa)* Mother believes you. You can go see Beulah fall off the cliff.

PENELOPE. *(Rises)* How are you going to punish Pops, Moms?

LAURA. God will take care of your Pops, dear.

PENELOPE. If God doesn't, *(Holding abdomen)* the stomachache will.

ACT I   EVERY FAMILY HAS ONE   35

(ESSIE *crosses from up* L. *to front door up* R.)

LAURA. Go upstairs and get ready for dinner. (PENELOPE *crosses by* LAURA *to* C. LAURA *lifts* PENELOPE'S *hair and looks behind her ears*) And remember your ears.
PENELOPE. *(Turns)* I washed my ears this morning!
LAURA. This time use *soap*. (PENELOPE *groans loudly—stamps foot—groans, and exits upstairs.* LAURA *crosses to end of sofa*) I'm all worn out and the company hasn't even arrived. *(Patting her hair)* If I had a mirror here I'd hate to believe it.
ESSIE. *(In the arch up* C.) The Parkers are here, ma'am—Mrs. Reardon.
LAURA. *(Rallying)* Good! *(As* ESSIE *exits up* L. MRS. PARKER *enters from up* R., *followed by her husband and* SHERWIN. MR. PARKER *is big and blustering and fifty.* SHERWIN *is twenty-five and good-looking in a plain way)* Hello, there! How marvelous seeing you again! Hello, Sherwin! *(She kisses him.)*

(MRS. PARKER *crosses behind sofa and sits on downstage end.*)

SHERWIN. *(Warmly)* Hello, Mrs. Reardon!
LAURA. *(With one hand in arm of each, looking from one to other as they come down)* Did you two big business men get everything attended to?
MR. PARKER. *(Proudly)* Everything came off splendidly. I let Sherwin handle most of the details and the boy acquitted himself nobly.
LAURA. *(To* MR. PARKER, *indicating the sofa)* Do sit down.
SHERWIN. *(Going to* NANA) How are you, Mrs. Reardon? But I suppose I'd better get in the habit of calling you Grandma.

NANA. *(With forced gaiety)* Ha, ha! And what shall I get in the habit of calling you?
SHERWIN. Why, whatever you like.
NANA. Remember I have your permission.
LAURA. *(Pointing to ottoman R.C.)* Sherwin.

(SHERWIN *sits on ottoman.*)

MR. PARKER. *(To LAURA)* Isn't Mr. Reardon home from business yet?
LAURA. He didn't go in town today. He wanted to take it easy.
NANA. He put the third floor bath out of commission, crossed the pipes in the kitchen sink and no one has dared look at the car.
MR. PARKER. I've got a lot to talk to him about, but if he doesn't feel well—
LAURA. *(Gets chair up L. and moves it down to up L.C.)* He's been taking medicine. He'll be all right later. *(Sits.)*
MRS. PARKER. Have *you* been a good boy about your medicine, James?
MR. PARKER. Haven't taken a pill for weeks, Bessie! I've never felt so fit.
MRS. PARKER. Oh, and they were such a pretty color.
MR. PARKER. *(In a loud whisper to LAURA as he looks across at NANA)* How's the old lady been doing?
NANA. *(Quickly)* If you mean me, I'm still breathing.
MR. PARKER. Eat regularly?
NANA. Yes, I can still swing a fork.
LAURA. Nana is the youngest in the family. She'll be with us forever.
NANA. *(Fervently)* Heaven forbid!
SHERWIN. And how is Marcia?

LAURA. *(Gushingly)* Too excited to eat or sleep. Oh, but she's happy!

MRS. PARKER. James tells me Sherwin has been in a positive coma. (SHERWIN, *bashful boy business*) Dear boy, it's his first marriage.

NANA. Who do you think Marcia is? Peggy Hopkins Joyce?

LAURA. *(Hurriedly)* Nana's not herself today. Been having a touch of her old complaint.

MR. PARKER. Sorry to hear that. *(To* NANA*)* What *is* your old complaint, Mrs. Reardon?

NANA. *(Sweetly)* People!

MR. PARKER. *(Puzzled)* People? *(Laughing heartily)* Ha, ha! I get it! Some kidder, eh, Grandma? Ha, ha!

(MRS. PARKER *doesn't "get it," so anticlimax laugh.* SHERWIN *joins in.* NANA *controls herself with effort.*)

LAURA. *(Eager to change the subject)* And how did you find business?

SHERWIN. Definitely a major pickup everywhere

MR. PARKER. Ten percent better for May than for April. And thirty percent more than for May of last year. Figures don't lie.

LAURA. And you want to let Reginald merge with you. Oh, you're so kind!

MR. PARKER. We're both in the canned foods business and since our children are marrying I think it would be wise to keep everything in the family.

LAURA. It would make everything so cosy, wouldn't it? And profitable, too.

MR. PARKER. Together we'd have the largest company on the market. Could afford extensive radio advertising and publicity. You can't doubt the advantages. After all, Parker & Company is one of the *oldest* firms there is.

NANA. *(Sharply)* We're not discussing a bottle of wine! We're discussing business and age has nothing to do with it—except when age *controls* it. *(Warningly)* Don't any of you forget that "Grandma" here owns fifty-one percent of the stock. I sold the first jar of Reardon preserves—and in my own kitchen, too.

LAURA. *(Rises and crosses to above table down R.C.)* Hush, Nana, darling. You know how to cook but you have no head for business.

MR. PARKER. That's right!

NANA. *(Rising. Crosses to slightly above MR. PARKER as LAURA goes R.)* I made Reardon & Reardon. My husband was out of a job and I sold jams. Pretty soon I had my husband selling them, too. And then we opened a store and then another store and the rest is history.

MR. PARKER. We know you're an admirable old lady but methods have changed. This is the day of big firms. The small fry haven't a chance.

NANA. *(Half step toward him)* We're doing all right, thank you. *(Meaningly)* And we shall continue doing all right. *(To LAURA—turns)* No head for business, eh? Have you forgotten the name they used to call me back in St. Peter's?

LAURA. *(Crossing to NANA)* Hush, Nana!

NANA. Don't worry, I shan't repeat it. *(Crosses to radio and looks at Bing Crosby album.)*

LAURA. *(Taking chair up to original position against back wall up L. Hurriedly)* Well—well, let's not discuss business *now.* *(Down to SHERWIN)* Sherwin, why not go upstairs and let Marcia know you're finally here? *(Coyly)* But do break it to her gently.

SHERWIN. *(Rises)* Not a bad idea. *(Crosses up C. and LAURA moves R.)* I'm so anxious to see her. *(Turns around to downstage)* If you'll excuse me—

ACT I   EVERY FAMILY HAS ONE   39

(Exits, getting luggage off up R. *and taking it up-stairs.)*

MRS. PARKER. *(As he exits)* Oh! *(Too thrilled,* I can just *taste* romance in the air. *(Sighing)* I feel like a bride again myself. Imagine, in three weeks the great event will take place.

NANA. *(Turns. Darkly)* Many a slip—

(WARRY *begins to come downstairs. He has changed into a blue suit but has neglected to do something with his hair.)*

LAURA. Nana, how ridiculous! *(Sits on ottoman)* What possibly could happen?

WARRY. *(Stopping in arch)* Well, hello! *(Coming down to shake hands with* MR. PARKER.*)*

MR. PARKER. Ah, here he is, the budding genius. *(They shake hands)* How are all the sonnets and love lyrics coming along?

WARRY. *(Drawing hand away. With distaste)* I write *books,* Mr. Parker.

MRS. PARKER. They say everyone has a book in his system. Always wanted to write one myself but never had the time. I suppose it's as well you get it out of your system when you're young.

WARRY. You make it sound like laying an egg.

MR. PARKER. Well, son, when you've given up your writing and you're looking for a job, come see me.

WARRY. Thanks, *(Crossing to* LAURA*)* but I'd be too old to work.

MR. PARKER. Suppose you're going to be another Zane Grey *("Zane Grey" stops* WARRY*)* or maybe write some Tarzan stories. You like Tarzan?

WARRY. *(Folding arms, drawing up as he turns. Shuddering)* No, I've always preferred Superman.

MR. PARKER. *(At a loss) Superman?* Who's he?

LAURA. *(Sweetly)* Oh, some character in Shakespeare, (WARRY *reacts away to up* R.) I guess. Warry adores Shakespeare. (*Politely. Rising*) But I'm sure you'd like to go upstairs and freshen up.

MR. PARKER. (*Rising*) Not a bad idea. Those Lackawanna tunnels are like coal mines. (LAURA *and* MRS. PARKER *both laugh as* MRS. PARKER *crosses to* C. *Turns to* NANA) Excuse us, Mrs. Reardon?

NANA. (*With a gentle smile*) Ah, but with pleasure.

MRS. PARKER. (*As she and* MR. PARKER *follow* LAURA *upstairs*) But, James, were you *ready* to give up those pills?

MR. PARKER. (*As they exit out of sight*) Haven't had a sick day in months, Bessie.

WARRY. (*Banging keys of piano and crossing down* R.) I'll give him a sick day! Tarzan! He must think I'm a great writer. (*Crossing below easy chair* R.C. *With dignity*) And here I am striving to put the spirit of America on paper.

NANA. (*Crossing to below* C. *of sofa*) Oh, was that what that book was about? (*Sits.*)

WARRY. Certainly. (*Crossing to* C.) Something that clamored for release, something that— (*Revolving movement with hands*) well, it just boiled up inside me.

NANA. And (*One revolution*) boiled over on your mother.

WARRY. (*Crossing to her*) Don't *you* think I captured the joys and sorrows of a typical household?

NANA. (*Hedging*) Well, sort of typical.

WARRY. My heroine, isn't she genuine? In the first chapter where she rebukes her father and (*Dramatizing—shoving*) shoves him into the well, (*Push down, then step down*) isn't that what you'd do under *those* circumstances?

NANA. Maybe, under those circumstances.

WARRY. Oh, I hope my readers feel the same way. *(Sits on arm of sofa.)*

NANA. I don't like her name.

WARRY. But it wouldn't be real if she had a glamorous name. She's got to be plain Aggie. And John, what a hero! At the end after he loses his arm *(Chop off arm)* you just know he and Aggie will get together.

NANA. After all, what's the loss of an arm or two compared to Aggie? *(Gently)* Warry, why don't you write about people you really know? Why don't you write about Fernwood?

WARRY. *(Jumping up)* This dull, colorless town? Nothing ever happens in Fernwood. There's no Aggie here!

NANA. And no John, either, thank goodness.

WARRY. *(Confidently and with gestures)* Wait until the publishers read them. And the critics. They'll compare Aggie and John to Romeo and Juliet—streamlined.

NANA. But, Warry, you mustn't hope too much for this first attempt of yours.

WARRY. When you have the talent nothing can stop you. *(Crossing up C., hands in pockets)* That's why the Parkers get me so mad. They think I'm a joke. *(Turns)* Some nut kid playing at being a—a Tolstoy. That's why my book *must* be accepted—to show them. *(Down to above ottoman. Angrily)* Golly, why did Marcia ever say yes to Sherwin Parker?

NANA. *(Calmly)* She hasn't married him yet.

WARRY. If anything is going to happen to prevent the wedding it had better happen fast.

NANA. Who knows what trick Fate has up his sleeve?

WARRY. *(Smiling at her and leaning toward her)* *His* sleeve? I thought Fate was a woman—with gray hair.

NANA. *(Gruffly) His* sleeve! *(Sighing)* I wish your mother approved of Todd.

WARRY. You can't trace his family back *(Fluttering arms out in take-off on* LAURA*)* to the Mayflower. His mother has to do the *(Pause—looks off* R.*)* family wash herself *(Sitting on ottoman)* but what of it? (MARCIA *and* SHERWIN *start coming downstairs)* You probably did, too.

NANA. Your grandfather was the richest man in St. Peter's. But he never would let anyone but me do his shirts.

MARCIA. *(Entering from upstairs with* SHERWIN. *She has changed to an informal dinner dress)* Nana, you knew Sherwin was here, didn't you?

NANA. But of course. We had quite a chat. And now, *(Up)* Warry, didn't you say you wanted me to hear some of your outline for the new book?

WARRY. What? *(Catching on. Crossing to her)* Oh, yes, of course.

NANA. Then read it to me in the study. (WARRY *crosses by* NANA *to study door)* Excuse us, please.

(WARRY *and* NANA *exit,* NANA *following.)*

SHERWIN. *(Looking after them. Stopping in their direction, scratching head)* It's silly of me but *(Turns back to* MARCIA*)* sometimes I think your grandmother doesn't like me.

MARCIA. *(Crossing* SHERWIN *and sitting downstage end of sofa)* Certainly she does. It—it just takes her a long time to warm up to people.

SHERWIN. Oh, is that it? Well, I'll give her all the time she wants. *(Crossing to her and sitting beside her)* Did you miss me, Marcia? You haven't told me.

MARCIA. Yes, naturally I missed you.

SHERWIN. *(Moving closer to her)* You didn't answer my last letter.

MARCIA. *(Lamely)* I—I knew you'd be back so soon.

SHERWIN. *(Pauses, then he looks around room and settles back on sofa as he says line)* Mother has enjoyed her visit here. She's so impressed with your family. And she has promised us the Parker medals for our children. *(Putting arm up on back of sofa—expanding a bit)* Our children should be very proud of those medals.

MARCIA. If we have children let's not make them little snobs.

SHERWIN. Why should they be snobs?

MARCIA. They will be if we drill their ancestry into them incessantly.

SHERWIN. But if they're related to the greatest names in history—

MARCIA. *(Rising and crossing to C.)* Just the same I don't want my children going about with—with a *(Turns to him)* sandwich board on their backs saying "my uncle did such and such at Bunker Hill."

SHERWIN. *(Rising)* Sandwich board? Bunker Hill? Marcia, don't you feel well?

MARCIA. *(To table R.C.)* Nervous, I guess. *(Turns and comes to C.)* Anyway, let's not quarrel about our children when we aren't even married.

SHERWIN. *(Stoutly)* My dear, *(Step toward her)* we'll never quarrel—never.

MARCIA. Oh, now, we're bound to quarrel every now and then. Just to clear the atmosphere.

SHERWIN. My mother and father never quarrel.

MARCIA. Then they're superhuman. I have a terrible temper. Oh, Sherwin, you don't know. I—I *(Dramatizing)* throw things and scream and—and I'm an absolute shrew.

SHERWIN. *(Worriedly)* You *are* upset today, Marcia.

MARCIA. I'm just warning you about my temper.

SHERWIN. *(Taking her hand and patting her back*

paternally) If it will make you feel better, I have a terrible temper, too.

PENELOPE. *(Enters from upstairs, dressed in her very best and wearing a hair ribbon. She looks at* SHERWIN'S *arm)* Oh—par-don me. *(Hurries to piano.)*

SHERWIN. *(Withdrawing his arm)* Hello, Penelope, *(Crossing to* PENELOPE*)* how are you?

PENELOPE. But definitely in the pink. *(Sits. Begins to play scales louder and louder.)*

SHERWIN. *(To* MARCIA*)* Cute little thing, isn't she?

MARCIA. *(Crosses down below sofa)* You'll see her all the time after we're married. *(Sits downstage end.)*

SHERWIN. I love children.

MARCIA. I hope you like the piano.

(PENELOPE *strikes a false note.)*

SHERWIN. *(Doubtfully)* Well— *(Crossing to above* R. *of sofa)* I always *did.*

MARCIA. *(Summoning her courage)* Sherwin, I— I hope we're not making a mistake.

SHERWIN. *(Steps down to end of sofa. Unable to hear)* What—what did you say?

MARCIA. *(Loudly to drown out the piano)* I said—

LAURA. *(Entering from upstairs through arch, followed by the* PARKERS*)* What *is* all the racket in here? *(At the piano)* Penelope, not *now!* (LAURA *crosses down to and* R. *of* R.C. *chair.)*

PENELOPE. *(Stopping scales)* Whenever I'm in the mood—

MR. PARKER. *(Going to* MARCIA*)* And how is my daughter-to-be?

MARCIA. Fine, thank you, Mr. Parker.

MR. PARKER. Hope you've got a kiss for an old man. (MRS. PARKER *sits on ottoman)* That is, if

ACT I   EVERY FAMILY HAS ONE   45

your Sherwin and my Bessie won't be jealous. *(He kisses her.)*

PENELOPE. *(Her elbow on the keyboard)* Oh, boy! *(Clucking.)*

MR. PARKER. *(Turning. Crossing up to her)* And how is little Penelope? *(Pats her head as she winces.)*

MRS. PARKER. She just gets bigger every time James sees her.

PENELOPE. *(Looking at her)* I'm not the only one.

ESSIE. *(Enters up L. and stands in the arch)* Well, folks, you might just as well come in. It's on.

(PENELOPE *jumps up and steps down* R.)

LAURA. *(Controlling herself)* Thank you, Essie. *(To* MR. PARKER *as she crosses to up* C.*)* She means dinner is served. *(As* ESSIE *exits* LAURA *turns)* Where are Warry and Nana?

MARCIA. In the study. *(Crossing to the study door)* I'll tell them. *(Opening the study door)* Dinner is ready.

MR. PARKER. *(To* PENELOPE, *patting her head again—same reaction.* MARCIA *comes back to below downstage end of sofa)* And do they let the little girl eat with the grownups every night?

PENELOPE. *(Backing away from him down* R.*)* Guess if I can stand it they can.

REGINALD. *(Enters through the arch from up* L. *carrying a telegram)* Good evening, everyone. Laura, this telegram just came for you.

(WARRY *and* NANA *come out of the study.)*

LAURA. *(Taking the telegram. Turns and steps downstage as she opens it)* Oh, but I hate these things.

MR. PARKER. *(To* REGINALD, *shaking hands)* And how have you been, Reardon?

REGINALD. Never better. How was the business trip?

LAURA. *(With a cry of alarm; crosses up* C. *to* REGINALD, *who meets her* C.*)* Oh—listen to this.

NANA. *(Going to her side.* WARRY *drops down beside* MARCIA*)* What is it? You're pale as a ghost.

LAURA. *(Reading the telegram aloud)* Will arrive shortly. Thanks for the invitation. Love to all. Lily.

NANA. *(Gasping)* Lily?! *(Takes telegram, crosses to upstage end of sofa and sits.)*

MARCIA. Who is Lily?

PENELOPE. Golly, she must be *somebody*. Mother has turned green.

(WALLY *and* MARCIA *murmur together.*)

LAURA. *(Hotly)* I am *not* green. And it was sent from Hoboken. That means any minute now— It must have been sent from the terminal—on her way here. *(WARN Curtain.)*

REGINALD. *(Thinking hard)* Lily? Lily? Say, is she who I think she is? (LAURA *nods vigorously. React upstage* R. *by bookcase)* Ohmigosh!

MRS. PARKER. This Lily sounds positively exciting. Who is she?

LAURA. *(Rallying)* She's a— She's a relative from St. Peter's. Lovely girl, really. So—so *unusual.* *(Looks at* NANA, *who nods an "I'll say!" nod.)*

PENELOPE. How shortly is shortly, Moms?

LAURA. *(Weakly)* I'm afraid any minute, darling. *(Recovering)* Come along, everyone. Dinner is ready. We must *eat*, regardless.

(LAURA *and* MR. PARKER *go out together, arm in arm.* REGINALD *and* MRS. PARKER *likewise.*)

MR. PARKER. *(As they disappear from view up* L.*)* I'm so hungry I could eat a team of horses—and without any gravy, ha, ha!

LAURA. *(Off up* L.*)* They wouldn't taste very good without gravy.

MRS. PARKER. *(To* REGINALD *as they exit)* I'm so anxious to meet one of your relatives from that lovely little town of St. Peter's. It sounds just heavenly.

MARCIA. *(As she and* SHERWIN *follow the others out)* I never even heard of Lily. I guess she must be a cousin.

WARRY. *(Exiting, following* OTHERS*)* Cousin Lily, she's certainly *news* to me.

PENELOPE. *(Starts to follow others out, but* NANA's *laugh stops her* C.*—she turns)* What's so funny, Nana?

NANA. Your grandmother has just decided that maybe *(Rises)* Fate is *(Crosses to* PENELOPE*)* a woman after all. *(Takes her arm. Vehemently)* And right now she's a woman with an empty stomach.

PENELOPE. Ha! Ha!

(And NANA *and* PENELOPE *start up* C. *as—)*

THE CURTAIN FALLS QUICKLY

End of Act One.

ACT TWO

The scene is the same, shortly after dinner that night. MUSIC coming from radio as Curtain rises. NANA is seated in her easy chair doing some needlework. MRS. PARKER and LAURA are seated on the sofa.

MRS. PARKER. *(Who can be heard as the Curtain rises)* Naturally when the society editor called on the phone I had to tell him all about the wedding. He was delighted to hear it first and promised to come out here and attend it *personally*.

LAURA. How too wonderful! Oh, it's going to be the most perfect wedding. I shall weep buckets and buckets. I always cry at weddings—and funerals.

MRS. PARKER. I wish we could have it in New York so that everyone could come.

LAURA. Marcia wants to be married right here in Fernwood. And, after all, it's *her* wedding.

NANA. Never know it.

MRS. PARKER. I wonder when those three big business men will be finished in the dining room? *(Leaning toward NANA)* Mrs. Reardon, I can't understand your reluctance to merge with Parker & Company.

NANA. Just an old woman's eccentricity.

MRS. PARKER. But it's not fair to your son. Why, with James managing most of the business Mr. Reardon would have time for all those little things like tennis and golf and polo—

ACT II   EVERY FAMILY HAS ONE

NANA. *(Laughing)* I can think of nothing funnier than Reginald playing polo.

MRS. PARKER. James plays.

NANA. Just the same I think Reginald would look funnier.

LAURA. *(Quickly)* Too bad Marcia has a headache. All the excitement, I guess.

MRS. PARKER. *(Dreamily)* I remember when I was engaged. James had to chase me all over Long Island before I said yes. When I did say yes he nearly collapsed.

NANA. Couldn't take it, eh?

MRS. PARKER. *(Rising uneasily. Crossing up C.)* I—I think I'll hurry the boys along. We *(On steps, turning)* do want to go for a little drive tonight. *(Exits through arch up L.)*

LAURA. *(Rises and crosses up C.)* Yes, do hurry them. *(Coming down to above table)* Nana, you're positively rude to the Parkers. Haven't I enough troubles with this—Lily about to *(Flings arm out)* burst on our heads any minute?

NANA. There's going to be a hot *(Snaps fingers)* time in this old town tonight.

LAURA. *(Up on step)* She's certainly slow in getting here. *(Hopefully)* Wouldn't it be wonderful if she's lost?

NANA. Not Lily. She's probably having too much fun to leave Hoboken.

LAURA. Now, *(Down off step in direction of NANA)* Nana, who could have fun in Hoboken?

NANA. Lily could.

LAURA. *(Tearfully. Crossing to turn off RADIO)* Oh, dear, and I haven't even an aspirin in the house. *(RADIO off.)*

NANA. We'll all need something that comes in a bottle but it isn't aspirin.

LAURA. *(Crosses to below sofa)* Even though I did send her an invitation, the nerve of her thinking that I meant it! *(Fixing pillow on sofa, then straightens up. In horror)* Do you suppose she still does those cartwheels whenever she's bored?

NANA. What I wonder is if she's bringing her husband, too.

LAURA. Nana, what a dreadful thought! *(Sinks on sofa, downstage end)* The Parkers are going to think no wonder we moved from St. Peter's with those monkeys staring us in the face.

NANA. I'll bet all their cousins don't look like Veronica Lake. *(Sharply)* It's too bad the Parkers can't meet one of our relatives without your having a breakdown.

LAURA. But this particular relative. She just walked down the street and women pulled their children in.

MRS. PARKER. *(Entering from up L., followed by* MR. PARKER, SHERWIN *and* REGINALD. MR. PARKER *crosses above* NANA *to down* R. MRS. PARKER *stands below ottoman.* SHERWIN *at* C. *with* REGINALD *at* L.C.*)* We're all going for a drive. Isn't that fun?

LAURA. Lovely idea! *(Stands)* Reginald, get the car ready.

REGINALD. *(Crossing to* LAURA*)* But—but, dear, I can't. I've been working on the car and—and—

LAURA. *(Freezing)* And what, Reginald?

REGINALD. Well, you see, the engine—

LAURA. Yes, Reginald, what about the engine?

REGINALD. Oh, there's nothing the matter with it, dear. It'll be fine—when I get it back in the car.

LAURA. Of all the times to play games with the engine!

MR. PARKER. We can use our roadster. We can sit on each other's lap. Ha, ha!

NANA. Ha, ha, yourself. *(Pulls needle through fabric at* MR. PARKER, *who gives* R.*)* I'm staying home.

LAURA. Yes, Nana, you stay here and greet Lily.

ACT II   EVERY FAMILY HAS ONE   51

(Crosses to NANA. SHERWIN *moves* L.*)* And be sure and send her right up to bed if she's tired. *(Crosses to* MR. PARKER. *As she takes his arm)* Shall we go?

MR. PARKER. Anxious to meet someone from that home town of yours.

(They exit French doors. MRS. PARKER *and* REGINALD *are following them out when* SHERWIN *stops them at French doors as he comes down* C.*)*

SHERWIN. Mother, *(They turn)* since there's only room for four, I'll stay here with Marcia.

NANA. But Marcia went upstairs with a headache. She's probably asleep.

SHERWIN. I want to be here when she wakes up.

MRS. PARKER. *(As she and* REGINALD *turn and exit through French doors)* My boy is so considerate!

SHERWIN. *(Smiling at* NANA, *who glares back at him)* Nice—nice night, isn't it?

NANA. *(Pause)* If you like nights.

SHERWIN. Don't you?

NANA. *(Pause. Drily)* Not so much as I used to. *(Puts needlework in basket on table.)*

SHERWIN. *(Crosses to French doors, leans against upstage door, looking out; coat open, hand in trouser pocket)* There's something about the moonlight. Something soft and—and romantic.

NANA. *(Pause)* Yes, so I remember.

SHERWIN. *(Keeps looking out)* If you didn't resist it might—well, it might *get* you.

NANA. *(Pause)* Do you resist?

SHERWIN. *(Turning, pulls hand out of pocket; buttons up coat)* Of course. Don't you?

NANA. *(Pause)* At my age could it matter?

SHERWIN. It's such a responsibility having a name like Parker to live up to. *(Sits on window-seat)* You can't do the things you'd like to. Once all I cared about was numismatics.

NANA. Numismatics? *(Drawing away from him)* Sounds like a disease.

SHERWIN. It's collecting rare coins. But Mother and Father talked me out of it.

NANA. *(Confidentially)* Frankly, young man, don't you often wish you were just plain John Smith?

SHERWIN. Oh, no. *(Rises)* I'm not one to shirk responsibilities. *(Reflectively)* But I guess John Smith could be a numismatician if he wanted to be.

WARRY. *(Coming out of the study—in to below upstage end of sofa)* No Cousin Lily yet, Nana?

NANA. So far so good.

SHERWIN. *(Crossing to* WARRY*)* You must read me some of your work sometime, Warry. I'm good at that sort of thing. I was on the school paper in college. *(Going up* C.*)* I've got some unpacking to do *(Turns)* if you'll excuse me. *(Hands in pockets, hums as he leaves. Exits upstairs.)*

WARRY. *(Crossing to* NANA*)* As though *he* could understand my message!

NANA. What have you been doing?

WARRY. *(Sitting on footstool at* NANA's *feet)* I've been in the study—musing.

NANA. *(Fondly)* And after all this musing what are your conclusions?

WARRY. Well, I was musing about life—and there are no conclusions. Gosh, one minute you're in the crib and the next minute you're going on eighteen. It's all so short. *(Desolately, head between hands)* What have I done with all my life?

NANA. People have to be out of their diapers before they set the world on fire.

WARRY. You know, suddenly I'm doubting myself. That's bad.

NANA. *(Rumpling his hair affectionately)* That's

good. It's a healthy sign, Warry. Cheer up! By morning you'll be—Shakespeare again.

WARRY. *(Doubtfully)* I don't know. Something's got me down.

NANA. You spend too much time in that study. You've sent one masterpiece off to the publishers, so before you start a new one have a vacation. It's spring, Warry, and when you're young in the springtime— *(Taps* WARRY's *shoulder)* aah!

WARRY. You mean fall in love?

NANA. There's nothing so much fun as *puppy love.*

WARRY. But I have no time for kid stuff. *(Hand to heart)* I have my career.

NANA. You're missing an awful lot. Besides, it would help you with your career. After all, you can't write about things you haven't experienced.

WARRY. *(Rising)* No, I'm never going to fall in love—again.

NANA. Again?

WARRY. *(Walking away. Crosses to up* C.*)* Oh, nobody knew. I concealed it. It shows what a good actor I am. My broken heart was my secret. *(Turns and comes down by bench)* Say, don't you remember a few months ago when I acted sort of funny?

NANA. You had a head cold, I remember.

WARRY. Oh, that was no head cold. *(Hitches up trousers) That* was love.

NANA. Who was she?

WARRY. *(Crossing* C.*)* She was a hunk of bone *(Hand pulled over face)* —a rag of hair— *(Turning and running fingers through hair from back of head to front.)*

NANA. Sounds too beautiful.

WARRY. *(Crosses to downstage end of sofa)* She was Cleopatra, Circe and—and *(Seductive pose on sofa)* Lucretia Borgia.

NANA. *(Rising, alarmed)* Young man, *(Crossing*

to below upstage end of sofa) who was this woman?

WARRY. Doris Howard.

NANA. Doris?—That little blonde with the *(Slight pause; flip fingers)* giggle on Sycamore Street?

WARRY. *(Dramatically)* But you don't know.

NANA. *(Sitting beside* WARRY*)* I've played bridge with her mother. You're lucky she turned you down.

WARRY. I turned *her* down. I read her some of my book and she laughed—*laughed*— *(Hand spread over heart, then clenching fist. Brokenly)* Something inside me just crinkled up and—and died. *(Elbow on knee; hand on fist. Grimly)* But I got even. I didn't dedicate my book to her.

NANA. *(Shaking her head)* That should teach her.

WARRY. She was an angel—and a devil. So from now on all I shall think about is my career. And you can give love back to the Indians.

NANA. Oh, someone else will come along and—

WARRY. *(Resolutely)* Oh, no—never again.

NANA. I *know*. Don't forget I was going on eighteen once myself.

WARRY. Who were you in love with?

NANA. *(Dreamily)* He was my geometry teacher. But he was beautiful. (PENELOPE *tears down stairs; stops up* C. *on steps; waves "Hi-yah!"; dashes to piano; starts pounding out scales)* Isn't it your bedtime?

PENELOPE. *(Playing the scales)* Moms said I could stay up until nine.

NANA. Do you have to bang that thing now? The Parkers aren't here.

PENELOPE. *(A business woman)* Of course if you'd make it interesting for me not to—

NANA. Is five cents interesting? (PENELOPE *plays louder)* Very well, a dime—but not a cent more.

PENELOPE. *(Stopping her scales)* Well, seeing that you're my only grandmother— *(Rising. As she*

ACT II   EVERY FAMILY HAS ONE   55

crosses to NANA, *holding out hand)* I think a dime *would* interest me.

NANA. My purse is on my bureau. Take Maudie to the Soda Bar and buy her a cone.

PENELOPE. *(With gesture of rejection)* I think that baby's in bed asleep.

NANA. Well, throw a pebble at her window and wake her up.

PENELOPE. *(Starting for slingshot on table down* R.C.*)* Good idea, Nana.

NANA. I said *pebble*. Not rock.

PENELOPE. Okey dokey! *(Turns and runs upstairs with slingshot.)*

NANA. That one takes after her grandmother. If there wasn't any trouble to get into I'd make trouble—and fast.

WARRY. And just look at you now, a *(Rising)* pillar of society.

NANA. Don't use that word society. It makes me think of the Parkers.

WARRY. *(Going to the study door)* Well, recess is over. I've got to get back to work.

(WARRY *goes into the study.* NANA *rises and goes to the radio-phonograph and selects a record. She puts it on. Record is Bing Crosby singing cowboy song—"I'm An Old Cowhand."* NANA *comes down* L., *swaying slightly to music.* NANA *is at* L. *when* ESSIE *crosses from up* L. *on way to front door.* NANA *crosses to her chair, doing modified version of latest dance step.)*

ESSIE. *(Returning as* NANA *gets to chair, after listening a minute, speaks, turns)* My, ain't that pretty! *(After a short pause in which she stands there enraptured)* Oh, I forgot. There's a Lily Reardon outside to see you.

NANA. Well, why didn't you tell me? Show her in.

(ESSIE *exits up* R. NANA *crosses to radio-phonograph, and begins to come down* L.; *hears* LILY; *turns, pats her hair and smoothes her dress as she comes toward downstage end of sofa.* ESSIE *carries* LILY'S *bag upstairs.* LILY *enters from up* R. *She is a pretty, vibrant girl of seventeen or eighteen. Tastefully dressed, she is a surprise to* NANA.)

NANA. Lily! *(Comes rest of way down to below end of sofa)* But *you're* not Lily.

LILY. Oh, yes. *(Coming down off steps to* C.) I'm Lily. You're—

NANA. *(Crossing toward her)* I'm Nana to everyone. But you're just a child. You can't be Lily.

LILY. *(Smiling)* You must have expected Mother. I'm Lily's daughter. Some friends of mine were driving to New York, so I thought I'd visit you. I—I hope you don't mind.

NANA. Mind? *(Crossing to* LILY, *kisses her)* We're delighted. Forgive me *if* I seem shocked but after all you're not what I expected. No, you're certainly not.

LILY. *(Turning around)* No more calico and braids in St. Peter's now, Nana.

NANA. Evidently not. But sit down, my dear— *(Taking her over to sofa)* and tell me all about St. Peter's. *(As they sit on the sofa)* Your mother—how *is* Lily?

LILY. Oh, Mother is the same as ever.

NANA. *(Flustered)* Oh, I'm sorry. Er—I mean—isn't that nice? And that man—I mean your father—how is he?

LILY. Father is the mayor now.

NANA. *Your* father—mayor? My stars, the town has changed.

LILY. *(Proudly)* You know all the things Father has done.

EVERY FAMILY HAS ONE

NANA. *(Uneasily, turning front)* Well, I know most of them.

LILY. The town just wanted to reward such an active citizen so they made him mayor. And Mother is still head of the Ladies League.

NANA. Still? *(Leaning back)* I never knew she belonged to the Ladies League.

LILY. My, yes. She's quite a leader. *(Making sweeping gesture)* She blazes a trail and the others follow. Some say she's a radical. What do you think?

NANA. Well, I always thought she was—well, *different*. Does she still run that funny little candy store?

LILY. Candy store? Mother never ran a candy store.

NANA. She did years ago. When your father was —well—when your father was away.

LILY. *(In horror)* Good heavens, you must be talking about *Lily*.

NANA. Certainly I'm talking about Lily. Who are you talking about?

LILY. Not *that* Lily. My mother is Lily Perkins.

NANA. Daughter of old Reverend Perkins?

LILY. Yes, he's my grandfather. My mother married your cousin Susie's son, Harry. And I'm their daughter.

NANA. Well, well, so Lily Perkins finally did marry Harry Reardon. Congratulations.

LILY. They were married twenty years ago.

NANA. But the other Lily? What happened to her?

LILY. She moved to—uh—*Buffalo*. She had to move to Buffalo. The town got up a petition.

NANA. The trouble with this family is too many Lilys in it.

LILY. I never thought that invitation was sent to

the other Lily. Gosh, why did you want *her* here? And at a wedding, too.

NANA. Laura didn't actually want her. She only wanted her to think she was wanted. *(Confidentially)* I was glad she was coming. *I* wanted her here.

LILY. But she'd disgrace you.

NANA. That's exactly why I wanted her here.

LILY. *(Puzzled. Moving uneasily)* You're sort of strange, too— *(Leaning toward* NANA*)* but I like you.

NANA. My dear, Marcia is marrying a boy she doesn't love. He's bad enough but his mother and father are invitations to murder. Since family and background are so important to these snobs, I was glad to show them our worst relative. I know no one could scare them away like Lily.

LILY. I'm sorry I disappointed you.

NANA. It was just a crazy whim on my part. And it's very nice having a charming little girl like you here.

LILY. I was so happy about coming. I'm not going back, Nana.

NANA. Not going back?

LILY. No, *(Stands. Crossing* C.; *turns)* I'm going to stay here and get a job on the stage. Mother and Father don't know it, but I'm going to be a great actress.

NANA. Have you ever done any acting?

LILY. Oh, my, yes! I was the lead in all the high school plays and I'm always head angel in the pageants. All I need is a little experience.

NANA. So all you need is a little experience?

LILY. Yes. Perhaps you know of some stock company somewhere.

NANA. *(With an idea. Up; crossing to* LILY*)* My child, you don't need a stock company. You can get all your experience right here.

LILY. I don't understand.

NANA Pretend you *are* Lily's daughter. The Buffalo Lily's daughter. Disgrace us with the Parkers. Tell terrible tales about the Reardons and St. Peter's. Oh, will you do it?

LILY. *(Slowly)* Act the way the daughter of Lily in Buffalo might act? (NANA *nods vigorously*) Why, they'd think there was insanity in the family.

NANA. That's what I want them to think.

LILY. *(Crossing by* NANA, *thinking)* It should be a wonderful experience—and lots of fun—and, anyway, I'm sick of being head angels. Yes, *(Turns)* I'll do it if you'll let me stay here and help me get a job.

NANA. I'll produce you on Broadway myself.

LILY. Oh, *(Turns and to* L. *slightly)* I'll show him.

NANA. Him? Who's *him?*

LILY. Someone back in St. Peter's. *(Sits on sofa)* Someone I never want to see again. When I told him I was going on the stage he *laughed*. He laughed *(Same action as* WARRY'S *on similar line)* and something within me just died.

NANA. St. Peter's, Brooklyn or Fernwood. I see it's the same the whole world over.

LILY. Love, I hate the word. From now on it's going to be my career alone.

NANA. Well, your career starts right here—and tonight. It's up to you to frighten those Parkers so much they never want to see anyone named Reardon as long as they live.

LILY. You want me to pretend that all the Reardons are a bit *(Finger in circular motion at temple)* nutty?

NANA. My dear, as *(Taps her temple)* nutty as a fruit cake.

LILY. And you don't care what I say or do?

AANA. Anything goes.

LILY. *(Excitedly. Up)* Oh, this is much more fun than a stock company.

WARRY. *(Coming out of the study; LILY turns)* Oh—hello! *(Looking at LILY admiringly)* Say, hello!

NANA. Warry, here's your Cousin Lily. (WARRY, *negative reaction)* Your fifth or sixth cousin.

WARRY. *(Immediately smitten)* How—how are you, Lily?

LILY. *(Fluttering her eyelids)* I'm just fine, thank you. Just perfectly fine. How are you?

NANA. *(Crossing to arch up C.)* You two can inquire about your health later. Lily, I'll show you to your room.

LILY. *(Following NANA)* I'll see you later, then, Warry.

WARRY. *(Tonguetied)* I'll—I'll be right here. *(Following them to landing at foot of stairs)* I'll be right here! *(After they exit upstairs he turns handspring from steps to down C.—ends facing French door.)*

(TODD GALLOWAY, *tall, good-looking, about twenty-two, suddenly appears in the French doorway.* WARRY *sees him as he straightens up.)*

WARRY. Why, Todd!

TODD. Warry, *(Step L.)* is Marcia home?

WARRY. *(Crossing to him)* Why, yes—yes, she's upstairs.

TODD. *(Crossing to sofa)* I'd like to see her alone for a few minutes.

WARRY. *(Going to him and stopping him)* Gosh, Todd, I don't think she will see you.

TODD. She's got to. I've got to talk to her.

WARRY. *(Hearing MARCIA and SHERWIN laugh, takes* TODD's *arm)* Get back, Todd—someone's coming. *(Pulls* TODD *across in front of him. Pushing* TODD *out of room through French doors)* Todd, wait outside and I'll see what I can do. I'll try to get Sherwin busy somehow or other. (TODD *exits and*

ACT II   EVERY FAMILY HAS ONE   61

WARRY *turns into room after partly closing French doors.* WARRY *whistles loudly as* MARCIA *enters from upstairs with* SHERWIN.)

MARCIA. Alone, Warry? I thought I heard you talking.

WARRY. Oh— *(Hand to head, still pacing)* oh, just talking to myself. Thinking out loud.

SHERWIN. Having trouble with your book?

WARRY. *(With a purpose. Up to* SHERWIN*)* Yes, that's it—the book. I'm stuck. There's a paragraph I just can't get right and you being on the school paper and all, Sherwin—

SHERWIN. *(Flattered)* If you're asking me to help you, I'd be glad to.

WARRY. *(Loudly, pushing* SHERWIN *ahead of himself)* Then suppose you and I go into the study for a few minutes, Sherwin.

MARCIA. Can't I come, too?

WARRY. *(Even louder, turning to* MARCIA*)* No, Marcia, you stay in here. You might disturb us.

MARCIA. You don't have to scream at me. I can take a hint.

SHERWIN. *(Throws line over shoulder as* WARRY *shoves him into study)* Won't be long, Marcia.

(WARRY *bangs door behind them.* MARCIA *looks puzzledly toward the study and then walks to get magazine from table* R.C. TODD *comes just inside French doors.* MARCIA *cries out with surprise.)*

MARCIA. Todd—!

TODD. Marcia, I had to see you. May—may I come in?

MARCIA. I'd— *(Starting up* C.*)* I'd rather you didn't.

TODD. *(Pleadingly)* For just a second?

MARCIA. *(Stops and turns)* Very well. For just a second. *(Crossing down to sofa)* What is it?

TODD. *(Crossing to* MARCIA*)* I had to see you before the wedding. That's why I came back to town.

MARCIA. *(Coldly)* Were you away? I don't remember your saying goodbye.

TODD. At the time I didn't think you cared whether I said goodbye or not.

MARCIA *(Turns and fires line sharply)* Why do you think I feel any different now?

TODD. I couldn't love you as much as I do without your caring for me—at least a little in return.

MARCIA. Oh, we've been through this so many times. *(Crosses R.)* Quarrels over trifles, both of us miserable—and then a reconciliation that never lasts. *(Sits easy chair R.C.)*

TODD. Because I was jealous of Sherwin, because your mother never wanted you to see me, because I didn't have a job. That's why we quarreled. *(Crosses up C.)*

MARCIA. I told you if you couldn't control your temper I never wanted to see you again. And then what do you do—have a brawl with Sherwin.

TODD. *(Crossing to above chair)* That's why I went away. Because you told me you never wanted to see me again.

MARCIA. *(Looking up at him)* A girl never means that. *(Quickly)* At least, sometimes she doesn't.

TODD. *(Angrily)* Then why did you get engaged to that piece of cheese right away?

MARCIA. *(Rises and steps toward* C.*)* He's *not* a piece of cheese, and *(Turns toward study)* even if he is I'll get engaged to any piece of cheese I want.

TODD. *(Groaning)* Here we go, fighting again.

MARCIA. It's all your fault. It always is.

TODD. And I suppose it's my fault the Galloways have no money and no important relatives?

MARCIA. *(Crossing to upstage end of sofa; sits)* I don't care about money or relatives.

TODD. But your mother does. *(Pause. Crosses to sofa)* If only I had something to offer. *(Sits on arm of sofa)* If only I had the *(Hands on her arms)* right to ask you to marry me.

MARCIA. *(Giving up to her heart)* I—I guess you don't have to offer me anything. You, just being you, is all that I want.

TODD. Then you do love me.

MARCIA. *(Soberly)* I'm not much good at pretending I don't.

TODD. *(Leans over and kisses her. Rises)* I was going to make a million dollars and throw it at your feet. *(Crosses)* And what did I get? A job selling brushes. *(Sits on sofa, L. of MARCIA)* But somebody said a mouthful when he said salesmen were born and not made.

MARCIA. But it's only for the time being. You have a future, Todd.

TODD. Yes, a black future. Oh, I'm just a dope, Marcia.

MARCIA. You've never had a break. But Todd, your break *will* come. It has to.

TODD. *(Bitterly)* Maybe by the time I'm ninety I'll have enough to support a wife.

MARCIA. Golly, what a mess I've got myself in. It would break Mother's heart if I don't marry Sherwin. And what about him? He loves me. At least, he's decided he's got to marry someone and it might as well be me.

TODD. I should have stayed away. But I haven't that brand of nobility. I was going to stand outside the house and watch for—for you—but I found myself walking right in.

MARCIA. I'm—I'm glad you did, Todd. So terribly glad. *(They are about to embrace again.)*

NANA. *(Entering from upstairs, smiling)* Why,

hello, there! (TODD *jumps up*) It's high time you paid us a visit, Todd.

MARCIA. *(Confused)* Nana, Todd was just passing by and—

TODD. Mrs. Reardon, I came uninvited. Marcia has nothing to do with it.

NANA. That's not the way it looked from where I was standing. So Marcia doesn't want you here, eh?

MARCIA. *(Heatedly, rising)* I do want him. *(Step toward* NANA*)* I love him, Nana! And he loves me. And I don't care what you or Mother or anyone says.

NANA. *(Sharply)* It's about time you came out in the open about it. *(Crosses to between* MARCIA *and* TODD. *With complete change of tone)* Well, (MARCIA *gives down* R.C.*)* what are your plans?

MARCIA. *(Amazed at* NANA's *reaction. A step toward* NANA*)* Plans?

NANA. I said plans! Or as usual is everything being left up to me? *(To* TODD*)* Don't know what this family would do without me. None of them got any spunk.

MARCIA. I'd marry Todd now if I could. *(Crossing* R. *below ottoman)* But I've got to think of other people as well as myself. Oh, Todd—please go.

TODD. *(Crosses to* MARCIA*)* This is my fault. As usual I've made everything worse. Good night, Mrs. Reardon. *(As he crosses her)* Goodbye, Marcia. *(He goes, partially closing French door.)*

MARCIA. *(Running to the French doors—opens door—calls)* Todd! *(She draws back; turns.)*

NANA. Well, why don't you go after him?

MARCIA. What good would that do?

NANA. *(Going to her)* Marcia Reardon, you're a fool.

MARCIA. *(Crosses by* NANA *and starts out up* C.*)* I'm all mixed up. Please don't rub it in.

NANA. *(Crossing to her)* You *are* a fool. *(Putting*

her arm around her) Asking him to go when you want him to stay. Right now your heart is out there chasing him down the street. *(Determinedly, crossing to below sofa)* Well, I see Grandma has some arranging to do.

MARCIA. *(Hopefully, to her)* Nana, *can* you do something?

NANA. Trust me, my child. The campaign, in fact, has been started already. There's nothing that I wouldn't do to keep you from marrying that—that— Boston bean.

(Sound of TALKING and COUGHING. MRS. PARKER and REGINALD enter French doors, followed by MR. PARKER and LAURA. MRS. PARKER crosses to ottoman. REGINALD drops upstage by MARCIA. who dropped up R.C. on their entrance.)

LAURA. *(Entering through French doors)* Oh, we did have a lovely ride! The moon was full. But Mr. Parker coughed so we had to come back.

MRS. PARKER. James, dear, *(Sits on ottoman)* don't you think you really should have a pill?

MR. PARKER. Nonsense, Bessie. *(Crosses to sofa)* I told you I was through taking pills. *(Sits.)*

LAURA. Nana, isn't it your bedtime?

NANA. *(Crossing to the easy chair)* Penelope isn't home yet. Guess I can stay up as late as she.

LAURA. She's probably with Maudie. *(Crosses to JAMES and sits at his R.)* Did I tell you, Mr. Parker, that the Winthrops live next door? *The* Winthrops. Their ancestors came over on the Mayflower.

MR. PARKER. I'll have to talk to them. The Parkers were on the Mayflower, too.

NANA. *(Thinking aloud)* From all the people who came over on it, that boat must have been bigger than the Queen Mary.

(MARCIA *laughs as she crosses down; pats* NANA'S *shoulders; then sits in window-seat.*)

LAURA. *(Hurriedly)* Well, now *(Settles on sofa)* didn't we have some business we wanted to discuss?

(REGINALD *crosses up* L. *to get extra chair.*)

MR. PARKER. Yes, we did. I'd like to explain a few things to Mrs. Reardon.
NANA. My answer is no (REGINALD *stops; puts chair down in place; turns to her)* to everything.
MR. PARKER. But shouldn't you at least listen to my proposition?
NANA. *(Stubbornly)* Save your words, Mr. Parker.
LILY. *(Coming downstairs.* REGINALD *gives* R. *to see who's coming. She is wearing a large flannel robe over a nightgown that must be* NANA'S) Yoo hoo Laura. *(Standing in arch.* MR. PARKER *stands.)*
LAURA. *(Stunned)* Did—did someone call me?
LILY. I did.
LAURA. *(Turning)* Who—who are you?
LILY. I'm Lily.
LAURA. *(Horrified; rises.* REGINALD *down to above table)* Heavens, monkey glands!
LILY. *(Still in the doorway)* Goodness, no. I'm Lily's daughter.
LAURA. *(Relieved)* Oh, her daughter! *(Crossing up to her almost.* MARCIA *rises and down* R. *Happily extending her arms)* Welcome, my dear. Welcome.
LILY. *(Comes down to* LAURA*)* Thank you, Laura. *(Kisses her)* I just feel perfectly at home already.
LAURA. *(Noticing the attire)* Yes, that's evident.
LILY. *(Sweetly)* Nana told me to make myself all comfy, so I did. *(Smiling at everyone)* Aren't you going to introduce me to all these perfectly charming people?

ACT II EVERY FAMILY HAS ONE 67

LAURA. Why, of course, my dear. This is Mr. Parker—

LILY. *(Going to* MR. PARKER *and shakes his hand vigorously)* Oh, Marcia's fiance! Isn't he just too handsome?

LAURA. *(As* MR. PARKER *blushes,* LAURA *coming down a step)* No, no, this is his father.

LILY. *(Turns to* LAURA*)* What? And so perfectly child-like? *(Turns to* MR. PARKER*)* I just can't get over it.

MR. PARKER. *(Clearing his throat)* How do you do, my child? How do you do?

LILY. *(Winking at him and giving him the "come-on")* Oh, I'm doing just fine—*now.*

LAURA. *(Indicating* MRS. PARKER. *Down step)* And this is Mrs. Parker.

LILY. *(Looks toward* MRS. PARKER*)* Ah, *(Looks toward* MR. PARKER*)* Mr. *(Looks toward* MRS. PARKER*)* Parker's *(Looks toward* MR. PARKER*)* mother.

LAURA. *(Alarmed)* Yes,— No, I mean this is Sherwin's mother.

LILY. *(Sadly, crosses and shakes hands with* MRS. PARKER—REGINALD *to* L. *above upstage end of sofa* —MR. PARKER, *hand to head, sinks onto sofa)* Oh, how do you do?

MRS. PARKER. *(Icily, withdrawing hand)* Quite well, thank you.

LILY. *(Sympathetically)* Just the same I wouldn't take any chances. *(To* NANA*)* It's her liver, isn't it?

LAURA. *(Steering her away from* MRS. PARKER. *Moves her below* MRS. PARKER*)* And here is Marcia.

(MRS. PARKER *gets up and crosses to* MR. PARKER.)

LILY. *(Kissing* MARCIA*)* Hello, Marcia! *(In a loud whisper to* LAURA*)* Doesn't look very cheerful for a bride.

LAURA. *(In haste)* And my husband, Reginald.

LIL. *(Going to* REGINALD. MARCIA, *puzzled and amused, crosses to sit on arm of* NANA'S *chair)* Oh, I can kiss you, can't I?

REGINALD. *(Beaming)* Don't see why not.

(LILY *leans up and kisses him while* LAURA *watches with displeasure.* MRS. PARKER *sits beside* MR. PARKER.)

LILY. So at last I meet Reginald. My, the stories they still tell about you in St. Peter's. *(Shaking her finger at him)* I'll bet you never told Laura about the time you courted Mother.

REGINALD. *(Surprised)* Me? Me, courting Lily?

LAURA. *(Bristling)* Indeed he didn't tell me. *(As* WARRY *and* SHERWIN *come out of the study)* Warry, have you met Lily?

WARRY. *(Enraptured. Going up* L.*)* I'll say.

LILY. *(Waving to him. Step toward him)* Indeed we have met. Why, we're practically old friends.

LAURA. And Marcia's fiancé, Sherwin Parker.

(LILY *crosses to* SHERWIN. WARRY *gives to above upstage end of table above sofa.* REGINALD *gives toward* C.)

LILY. *(Going to him, fluttering her eyelids)* At last!

SHERWIN. *(Nervously, his back against study door)* Hello—hello, there!

LILY. *(Across to* MARCIA. *With stiff fingers, punctuates line by poking on his chest)* I think he's the cutest thing outside of Tyrone Power.

LAURA. *(Uncomfortably, crossing down* C.*)* Shall —shall we all go for a drive or something?

MRS. PARKER. We just came back.

LAURA. Did we? Oh, yes, so we did. *(Turns and*

starts toward bookcase up R. WARRY *and* REGINALD *give* L.) Well, shall be play bridge?
  LILY. *(Excitedly, crossing to* C. SHERWIN *comes in to end of sofa almost)* Oh, no, let's *talk.*
  LAURA. *(Crossing down to ottoman)* Your dear mother, *(Sinks onto ottoman)* how is she?
  LILY. *(Standing* C.) Not so good lately. Her old trouble, you know.
  REGINALD. What *is* her old trouble?
  LILY. *(Simply)* Pa. But he'll be getting out in a year.
  REGINALD. Oh, has he been away?
  LILY. Yes, but not for so long this time. He had a good lawyer.
  LAURA. *(Quickly)* How is dear, dear St. Peter's?
  MR. PARKER. Yes, Mrs. Parker and I are dying to hear about St. Peter's.
  LILY. *(Crossing down to* PARKERS; REGINALD *drops down above* LAURA*)* It's the same old town. But they're going to pave the streets soon.
  MRS. PARKER. No—no pavements?
  LILY. No, they've been saving up for a schoolhouse.
  LAURA. *(Hopefully)* Aren't you tired after your long trip?
  LILY. No, *(Back to* C.*)* it's only half past eight. At home we always stay up until nine.
  LAURA. *(Appealingly, nodding vigorously)* Nana, shouldn't we insist that the dear child get some rest?
  NANA. *(Shaking head)* Nonsense. Let her stay up. *I'm* having a wonderful time. Tell me, Lily, how is the old Reardon home?
  LILY. Still next door to the glue factory. But there have been complaints and any day now they're going to have it moved away.
  MR. PARKER. The—the glue factory?
  LILY. No, the old homestead. We make a lot of noise and it disturbs the horses.

MRS. PARKER. How dreadful! Horses! Glue!

LILY. The horses never bother me. It was—the glue. *(Holding nose daintily.)*

MR. PARKER. St. Peter's doesn't sound like the town I thought it was.

LAURA. *(Rising)* But you men wanted to discuss business.

MR. PARKER. Yes, but I think this should prove interesting.

LAURA. Now, you gentlemen don't have to entertain Lily. *I'll* take care of her.

MR. PARKER. *(Rising)* You'll excuse us, Miss Reardon?

LILY. *(Beaming at him and waving)* Well, if you don't stay away *too* long.

MR. PARKER. *(Reluctantly)* Very well, then. (MR. PARKER *exits to study)* Come along, Sherwin.

(SHERWIN *exits to study.)*

REGINALD. *(Shaking his head as he crosses to study)* Imagine that glue factory still being there.

(He turns at door to look at LILY; she coyly flirts with him; he reacts and exits into study, closing door. LILY *goes up to* WARRY.)

MRS. PARKER. *(Rising, offendedly)* I think *(Crossing to up* C.) I shall go look for my *headache tablets.*

LAURA. Mrs. Parker, *(Going up to her)* may *I* borrow one? *(On steps as* MRS. PARKER *goes upstairs)* Come with me, Marcia. (MARCIA *rises)* Nana must have a lot to say to Lily. *(Meaningly)* Haven't you, Nana?

NANA. *(Chuckling)* You don't know!

MARCIA. *(Crossing up* C. *and out—upstairs)* See you later, Lily.

LAURA. *(On the stairs)* Come, Marcia.

(MARCIA *and* LAURA *go out of view upstairs.)*

NANA. *(To* WARRY*)* Warry, I—I left my *New Yorker* in the study. Will you go look for it?
WARRY. *(Crossing down to study)* Sure, Nana. *(At the study door)* Don't go away, Lily. *(He smiles at her, sighs, enters the study.)*
LILY. *(Crossing to* NANA*)* How am I doing?
NANA. *(With glee)* The American Theatre doesn't know what it's got in store.
LILY. And that was only the beginning.
NANA. I'll bet you're something when you really get warmed up.
LILY. And all the other things I've heard about the Reardons. I'll tell them, too.
NANA. *(Anxiously)* Don't overdo it. They'll become suspicious.
LILY. I haven't told one fabrication so far.
NANA. They must have pavements back in St. Peter's now.
LILY. *(Hedging)* Well, they're on the other side of the tracks. *(Confidentially)* But the glue factory was torn down six years ago.
WARRY. *(Entering from the study)* Your *New Yorker* wasn't in the study, Nana.
NANA. *(Feeling underneath her, pulls magazine out from under her; puts it on table)* My goodness, I've been sitting on it all the time. *(Rising)* Well, I don't want to read now anyway. I'll get myself a glass of milk. *(Crossing up* C.*)* Entertain Lily, Warry. I have a notion you two have a lot in common. *(In the arch)* Anyway, you've both got beautiful imaginations. Be nice to him, Lily, and maybe he'll write a play for you. *(Exits up* L.*)*
LILY. *(As* NANA *exits)* Oh, do *you* write? Write plays?
WARRY. *(Modestly, crossing to her)* Well, I haven't gotten around to plays—just yet.

LILY. Oh, but you've got to write a play. You see, I'm going to be an actress.

WARRY. *(Impressed, snapping fingers)* That's it! The minute I saw you I could tell you had a driving force.

LILY. I could tell you were—different, too.

WARRY. *(Studying her)* You know, you've got something none of the girls in Fernwood have. It's— it's that air of mystery.

LILY. *(Sadly, crossing to easy chair R.C.)* That's easily explained by my background. *(Sits)* You know about Mother and Father, don't you?

WARRY. *(Embarrassed)* Well, I didn't—until tonight. And now I've got a pretty good idea. *(Quickly, sits on ottoman)* But they *must* be nice people. I mean, to have a daughter like you.

LILY. And don't you hold it against me?

WARRY. *(Nobly)* Why should I blame you because your parents are a couple of black sheep?

LILY. *(Dramatically)* At last to meet someone who understands!

WARRY. *(Admiringly)* A child of tragedy, that's you. Most actresses are.

LILY. Are what?

WARRY. Children of *tragedy*. You've got to suffer if you're going to act or write.

LILY. Have you suffered, too?

WARRY. *(Looking away)* I guess when it comes to suffering you and I have a lot in common.

LILY. If I'm not too personal, what do you suffer best about?

WARRY. *(Sadly)* Love.

LILY. Unrequited?

WARRY. Quite unrequited. Of course, it was an experience. I'll never love anybody else, at least— never love anybody else so blindly again.

LILY. Love has made me suffer, too. He read me *poetry*. And then that lisping blonde came along.

WARRY. *(In horror, standing and reacting L.)* Don't mention blondes to me!

LILY. Was she a blonde?

WARRY. Very. *(Half turning away)* That beautiful gold.

LILY. *(Primly)* That shade gets dull very quickly.

WARRY. *(Turns to her)* When I'm the greatest writer in America she'll be sorry.

LILY. Perhaps she's sorry now.

WARRY. No. I saw her downtown yesterday. *(Sinks on arm of sofa)* She—she stuck out her tongue.

LILY. *(Up and crossing to him)* Don't waste any more thought on her. I'm not thinking about *him*. But when I'm a famous stage star I'll come back and haunt him.

WARRY. You know, with your background of suffering you should become a great emotional star.

LILY. But I've done so much suffering in real life that I want to be happy on the stage. I prefer comedy.

WARRY. *(In distaste. As he rises she gives R.)* Comedy? Anybody can do comedy. I think you'd make a great tragedienne. *(Determinedly. He steps toward her)* Say, if they ever make a play out of my book you must be Aggie.

LILY. *(Baffled)* Aggie? Who is Aggie?

WARRY. Another child of tragedy. *Ethereal,* elusive, long suffering—*you.*

LILY. *(Coquettishly)* I'll bet you tell every girl she's Aggie.

WARRY. No—just *her*. But she thought it was a joke. You should have heard her *laugh* when she read my book. Aggie wouldn't have laughed.

LILY. Evidently poor Aggie has nothing to laugh about.

WARRY. But you're going to be able to laugh from now on. Nobody here knows about your family.

Anyway, nobody here can afford to talk, anyway. *(Awkwardly reaches out)* Oh, you'll—you'll be *(Takes hold of her wrist)* glad you came.

(LAURA *and* MRS. PARKER *are seen starting downstairs.*)

LILY. Are—are you glad I came?
WARRY. *(Catching his breath)* Gee, Nana was right about "going on eighteen in the spring." *(Starts to get set to kiss her.)*
LAURA. *(Standing in arch)* Oh! *(As* LAURA *comes down steps.* WARRY *puts hands in pockets and crosses down* R., *whistling.* LILY *sits on ottoman.* MRS. PARKER *begins to cross to study, above table and down)* Are you still up, Lily?
MRS. PARKER. *(Crossing to the study)* I'm going to retire. I have some letters to write. *(Opening the study door and calling)* James, I'm going upstairs. *(Comes to front of sofa.)*
LAURA. Did you and Warry have a pleasant talk, Lily?
LILY. **Oh, yes, all about the family—and other things.**
LAURA. *(Up a step and part turn. Worried)* Oh, dear!
MR. PARKER. *(Coming out of the study with* REGINALD *and* SHERWIN*)* Going upstairs so early, Bessie?
MRS. PARKER. Yes, it's been a hectic day. You must be tired, too, James.
MR. PARKER. Tired, nonsense! You must think I'm an old man. I never felt better. *(Indicating* LILY *and crossing towards her and by* MRS. PARKER*)* This child has come all the way from Maine and she isn't tired.
LILY. I was so anxious to get out of St. Peter's I'd have walked here.

ACT II   EVERY FAMILY HAS ONE   75

LAURA. Really, Lily, the way you talk you make St. Peter's sound backward.

LILY. Well, since they repealed prohibition St. Peter's hasn't been exactly thriving.

MR. PARKER. They—they manufactured liquor?

LILY. Sure, in the kitchen. And delivered it, too.

MRS. PARKER. *(Sinking on the downstage end of couch.* LAURA *crosses up* R.C.; SHERWIN *drops up* L.*)* Bootleggers!

LILY. *(Proudly)* But nothing could daunt my father, dear soul! When there wasn't any money to be made in liquor he just sat himself down—and made money.

MR. PARKER. *(Interested, crossing to her)* I admire his initiative but how did he make money?

LILY. He just rigged up a machine and made it.

MRS. PARKER. *(Gasping)* You mean—he was a—a counterfeiter?!

LILY. He called it—artistic engraving.

(MR. PARKER *swings around and goes to above upstage end of sofa.)*

LAURA. *(Crossing down to* LILY*)* Lily, you'd—you'd better go to bed. You're so tired you're *raving*.

LILY. *(Sweetly)* I guess I am getting sleepy. *(Up and crosses to* MR. PARKER. *Running her fingers up his chest)* I'll see you in the morning, cutie-pie, and tell you heaps more about our funny family.

MR. PARKER. *(Gruffly)* I'm anxious to hear.

LILY. *(Crossing to* WARRY*)* Good night, Warry.

WARRY. *(Staunchly)* Good night, Lily. Remember we're *both* children of sorrow. (LAURA *and* REGINALD *look at each other. The* PARKERS *look at each other)* We'll keep our chins up together. (WARRY *takes* LILY'S *hand.)*

LILY. *(Taking his hand)* And forget the past—together. The worst is over. *(They step back one step, still holding hands)* Courage, comrade. *(They shake hands—three elaborate shakes.)*

(Too much for MR. PARKER, *who crosses far up* R.C., *watching what* LILY *and* WARRY *are doing.)*

MRS. PARKER. *(Watching them confusedly)* What *are* they talking about?

LAURA. *(Unhappily, crosses to* MRS. PARKER*)* She should never have been left alone with him. Maybe it's contagious. *(Sits on sofa beside* MRS. PARKER.*)*

LILY. *(Smiling at everyone, as she crosses up to steps)* Good night, all. *(Stands in the arch up* C. *as* NANA *enters)* I'm going to bed, Nana dear. Good night.

NANA. Good night, my child. I hope you're going to enjoy your visit here.

LILY. Oh, it's so wonderful to get away from that place, to forget for a while. *(Kissing* NANA*)* And I'm so relieved to see you looking so well.

NANA. *(Suspiciously)* Now what?

LILY. *(Innocently)* We were worried when you sent Mother that odd present last Christmas.

NANA. *(Sweetly)* What *odd* present, dear child?

LILY. Why, you remember. *(As she says each syllable, she jumps downstage as if on pogo stick)* That pogo stick— *(Stops—gesture)* covered with whipped cream.

NANA. *(Weakly)* Pogo stick?

MR. PARKER. *(Stepping toward her)* Covered with —with what?

MRS. PARKER. Whipped cream, dear. How very peculiar.   *(WARN Curtain.)*

LILY. Reminded me of one of Aunt Nellie's pranks. *(Shooting line to* LAURA, *who shakes head "no" vigorously)* Remember the time she put the paprika on her face and pretended she was an In-

ACT II   EVERY FAMILY HAS ONE   77

dian? *(Hops up in air as she lets out a war-whoop— one hand behind head with finger up for feather, other hand patting mouth for war-whoop as she hops down* C. *and below sofa to* REGINALD. *She hits him in abdomen as she goes by him—he doubles up. Then up toward* SHERWIN, *who backs upstage as she approaches. She goes to above upstage end of table, where she stops and eyes* MR. PARKER*)* Why, *(Marching down to* MR. PARKER, *who sinks onto ottoman)* she ran down Main Street just *(Grabs his hair with one hand and makes scalping motion with other)* screaming for a scalp.

(MR. PARKER *feels to see if scalp is still there.)*

MRS. PARKER. What—what happened?
LILY. Oh, they caught her before she'd done any harm. At least they caught her *that* time.
MR. PARKER. *(With handkerchief wiping his forehead)* She—she sounds sort of cuckoo to me.
LILY. Mad as a hatter, Mr. Parker. *(With a sigh. Wags her index finger at him with various movements up and down, back and forth, each movement punctuating a word)* As Mother says, there are more outside the booby hatch than there are inside. *(Turns and shoots line vigorously at* LAURA *and* MRS. PARKER*)* Why, the person sitting right next to you might be a trifle pixilated. In fact he probably is. (LAURA *and* MRS. PARKER *look at each other, then away as* LILY *goes up on landing and turns. In the arch up* C.*)* Good night again. *(And with a little wave to* EVERYONE *she exits upstairs.)*

(NANA *waves back and drops to above table down* R.C. WARRY *to above chair.)*

LAURA. *(Rises)* Paprika? *(Crosses up to steps, looking after* LILY*)* Scalps? *(Turning and crossing* *down to* c. *above table—line to* REGINALD) Who is Aunt Nellie?

REGINALD. I—I don't know. Who is she, Nana?

NANA. *(Sadly)* I don't want to tell you—*now.*

LAURA. *(Desperately, shouting line to* MRS. PARKER *and* SHERWIN, *last of it to* MR. PARKER) The—dear girl is so excited she doesn't know what she's saying. *(Trying to smile. Standing* C.) It's all a joke of some sort. *(Clearing* L. *for* PENELOPE. *Very forced laugh)* Ha, ha, ha!

MR. PARKER. *(With no conviction)* Yes, ha, ha! *(They* ALL *laugh uncomfortably. There is the sudden CRASH of breaking glass offstage.* PENELOPE *comes skipping in through the French doors, hands her slingshot to* MR. PARKER *and then tears upstairs.* MR. PARKER *looks dazedly at* MRS. PARKER, *then rises, a changed and aged man—saying, as he staggers toward sofa, still holding up slingshot as if poison—*LAURA *drops* R., MRS. PARKER *rises,* SHERWIN *comes* C. *around table, and* WARRY *drops down)* Bessie, Bessie—where are my pills?! *(Fainting onto sofa as—)*

THE CURTAIN FALLS QUICKLY

ACT THREE

It is the next morning and the French doors are opened, sunlight streaming in on the breakfast table. For this Act, the drop-leaf gate-leg table is set for breakfast. There is service for eight persons. NANA'S *easy chair is placed at the down* R. *side of the table. The ottoman is moved below the table. A dining-room chair is already placed down* L. *of the table.* ESSIE *later carries in two more dining-room chairs which she places below the table* R. *of the ottoman and up* R. *of the table above the easy chair. The other places are provided by the piano bench which* LAURA *moves into place and by the odd chair from up* L. *which* WARRY *sets at the* L. *upstage side of the table. The sofa and davenport table are moved from their almost straight front position to a slanting position at* L.C. NANA *is arranging the napkins as the Curtain rises.*

ESSIE. *(Entering from up* R. *with a letter)* That Galloway fellow just left this for Miss Marcia.

NANA. Oh, let me see it. *(Takes the note.* ESSIE *goes out up* L. NANA *hurriedly goes to the window in the hall up* C. *She calls as she looks out up* R.*)* Todd —oh, Todd Galloway! Come here a minute. *(Drops to* L. *of arch, looking at letter.)*

TODD. *(After a second appears from up* R.*)* Yes, Mrs. Reardon?

NANA. *(Holding up the letter)* I suppose this is one of those goodbye forever things?

TODD. In a way. (NANA *tears it up as she crosses down L. to above table. He comes down into room as he says*) Why did you do that?

NANA. Because there's no reason why Marcia should be caused any more grief. The poor girl is a nervous wreck, anyway. *(Vehemently)* She loves you, lad.

TODD. *(Crossing R.; stops as NANA speaks)* She'll get over it.

NANA. *(Following him)* No, she won't. It's the real thing. I can tell.

TODD. I can't ask her to give up Parker for me. I haven't a dime—nor an ancestor.

NANA. *(One step toward him)* No one cares about family except Laura. And something tells me that after today she won't do much talking.

TODD. But I can't support a wife on my salary. I've got the only job I could get—selling brushes.

NANA. *(Rest of way to him)* You're no dumbbell, Todd. And I believe in you. My husband didn't have a cent when I married him. Together we built up a good-sized business. Well, fifty-one percent of that business is still in my name.

TODD. Yes, but what's that got—

NANA. I'll tell you what it has to do with you. We can use a bright young man at the office. Warry doesn't give a hang for all the commerce in the world. Reginald would rather tinker any day. I'm willing to put you in and let you work.

TODD. Gosh, Mrs. Reardon, if only you would!

NANA. I'm going to. I want you to go into New York this morning. I'll telephone to the business manager about you. You start today.

TODD. I wish I knew what to say.

NANA. Don't say anything. *(Starting him out to French doors R.)* Get into town now. And tonight you can tell Marcia the good news.

TODD. *(Below table R.C.)* You're swell to do this!

NANA. Nonsense. Doesn't cost me anything. And you know how I feel about those Parkers. Good luck, Todd. *(Shaking hands.)*

TODD. So long—and thanks.

(TODD *goes out through the French doors as* WARRY *enters from up* L.)

WARRY. Wasn't that Todd?

NANA. Don't know. Was it?

WARRY. Sure did look like him. You taking Marcia's boy friend away?

NANA. Young man, you mind your own business. *(Crossing to sofa.)*

WARRY. *(Turning and a step toward* NANA. *Meaningly)* I have a hunch fate has something else up her sleeve.

NANA. *(Sitting on upstage end of sofa)* Oh, go in and write a book.

WARRY. *(Crosses to her)* You pretend to be so crotchety but you're just a *(Chucking her under chin)* cupid underneath.

NANA. *(Hitting his hand away)* Cupid, nonsense!

WARRY. Well, someone has been throwing love darts around. I got hit myself. *(Happily)* Isn't Cousin Lily a wow? *(Hitting his fist in his hand as he turns around, moving* R.)

NANA. She's a humdinger!

WARRY. *(Leaning against chair at* L. *of table)* If you could have seen your face last night! And the way the Parkers looked at you!

NANA. *(Grimly)* Pogo stick—with whipped cream! I'll pogo stick her!

WARRY. Cousin Lily got even with this family all right.

NANA. She's hardly related at all. Stop calling her "cousin."

WARRY. I'm glad of that. *(Stepping and turning down* C. *Casually)* I guess I was a bit hasty when I said I was through with love. I'll probably fall in love again—eventually.

NANA. Eventually—why not now?

WARRY. That's what I was thinking. *(Reflectively)* Poor tragic Lily, someone's got to make her happy. She's never had a chance. People have been terrible to her. It's not *her* fault how her father made his money. *(Crossing to* NANA. *Down to earth)* What do you think Mother will do to her?

NANA. I know she'd *like* to roast her on a spit over a slow fire. *(Turning a sofa pillow by the ends to illustrate.)*

LILY. *(Entering from upstairs)* Hello, Warry! (WARRY *drops up)* Good morning, Nana!

NANA. Don't you Nana me, young lady!

LILY. *(Crossing to* NANA. *Brightly)* My, you sound just positively perturbed about something.

NANA. Anyone accused of sending such a Christmas present has a lot to be perturbed about.

LILY. Oh, I was just trying to tease you.

NANA. I'll bet you put tacks on sofas and pull hairs away.

LILY. After all, the family *is* as nutty as a fruit cake.

NANA. *(Anxious to talk to her alone)* Warry—er—my *New Yorker*, it must be in the study. Will you look for it?

WARRY. *(Wearily, crossing toward study)* You're always losing the *New Yorker*.

LILY. *(Quickly, crossing after him; he turns)* I'll help you look for it, Warry.

WARRY. That'll be swell.

LILY. *(As she and* WARRY *are at the study)* We'll find it right away, (WARRY *turns and out)* Nana—if it's in here. (LILY *turns and out.)*

ACT III   EVERY FAMILY HAS ONE   83

(As they enter the study NANA *rises; shakes her fist after* LILY. SHERWIN *enters from upstairs and watches* NANA *as she shakes her fist.* NANA *senses his presence; turns and glares at him, then starts* R.*)*

NANA. Well?
SHERWIN. *(Looking at her clenched hand)* Good morning, Mrs. Reardon. *(Comes down to* R. *of table.)*
NANA. *(Limply)* I—er—my hand—it's asleep. *(Flips fingers out at him)* Yes, sound asleep.
SHERWIN. *(Uneasily)* Is—it is?
NANA. *(Crossly)* Well, what did you think I was doing? A Fascist salute? *(Kicking one foot up a bit. Crossing toward him, kicking foot as he gives* R.*)* Sometimes my foot goes to sleep, too.
SHERWIN. How—how inconsiderate. *(Edges away another step.)*
NANA. *(Annoyed)* Stop looking at me as though you thought I were crazy!
MARCIA. *(Entering from upstairs)* Good morning, Nana! Hello, Sherwin! *(She crosses to* NANA *and kisses her)* Isn't this a beautiful morning?
NANA. Please excuse me. I have some phoning to do. *(Turning in the arch up* C.*)* And, Sherwin, I still say anyone's hand can go to sleep. *(She sails out up* L.*)*
SHERWIN. *(Crossing up to steps; looks after her—then down to* MARCIA*)* There's a phone right there on that table. *(Turning and pointing to hall phone and table.)*
MARCIA. Probably something very private. Sherwin, I'm sorry about last night. Mother told me what Lily said. I don't understand it.
SHERWIN. *(Step toward her)* Neither do I. But your mother told us before she arrived that she was, well—unusual.

MARCIA. But I don't know if any of the things she said were true.

SHERWIN. *(Going to her)* I'm sure she was just making them up.

MARCIA. Why on earth should she?

SHERWIN. She might just be—well, funny that way.

MARCIA. For all you know we all may be funny that way. *(Crossing to front of table, pushing in chair)* How do your mother and father feel about this?

SHERWIN. *(Step R.)* Naturally they feel the same as I do. There's some mistake.

MARCIA. I've always heard such beautiful stories about St. Peter's. *(Give to R. slightly)* The majesty of the family home, the fine relatives— *(Turning back to him)* No one ever mentioned a glue factory or—or bootleggers or crazy Aunt Nellie.

SHERWIN. *(Crossing to* MARCIA. *Suddenly)* I have it!

MARCIA. You have what?

SHERWIN. Maybe she's in the wrong house.

MARCIA. That's hardly intelligent, Sherwin.

SHERWIN. Well, it's optimistic.

MARCIA. *(Giggling)* You know, I'm beginning to think it's funny.

SHERWIN. *(Watching her laugh)* I don't think it's *that* funny.

MARCIA. Oh, but it is! I may be marrying you under false pretenses.

SHERWIN. *(Nobly)* It's you I'm marrying, Marcia—not your family.

MARCIA. *(Soberly)* I wonder if you mean that.

SHERWIN. Why—why, of course I do!

MARCIA. Thank you for saying that, Sherwin. *(Crossing to French doors and turning)* I'm going to pick some flowers. Like to help?

ACT III EVERY FAMILY HAS ONE

SHERWIN. *(Crossing to her side as she starts out)* Of course. I'd be glad to.

(They go outside as ESSIE *enters from up* L. *She carries in two dining chairs for the table.* ESSIE *is in a cheerful mood and indicates it by singing.)*

ESSIE. *(Lustily as she places one chair front of table at* R. *of ottoman and the other at* R. *of table above the easy chair)* Oh, you made me what I yam today. I hope ye're satis-fied. You dragged me down and down and— *(The* PARKERS *enter from upstairs, interrupting the concert)* Morning, folks!

MR. PARKER. Good morning, Essie!

ESSIE. *(As she exits up* L. *she looks over the* PARKERS, *singing)* You dragged me down—and down—and down!

MR. PARKER. *(Waits for* ESSIE *to go, then crossing to table above sofa, picks up newspaper)* No, Bessie, I've decided. I don't go into town today. I'm going to stay here and watch these people.

MRS. PARKER. *(Slightly to* R., *thinking)* But I know that girl must have been—talking in her sleep or something.

MR. PARKER. *(Firmly)* Well, I'm going to stick around and hear the rest of her sleep-talking.

MRS. PARKER. *(Crossing and sitting on the sofa)* I couldn't sleep a wink last night.

MR. PARKER. Did I snore?

MRS. PARKER. No. I was just thinking.

MR. PARKER. So was I.

MRS. PARKER. But I'm *sure* there must be some mistake.

MR. PARKER. I'm sure of that, too. I only hope we aren't the ones who made it. *(Noticing the table. Crossing and pointing with newspaper)* I say, what's the breakfast table doing in here?

MRS. PARKER. *(Looking at it)* I don't know. But there must be some reason.

MR. PARKER. She probably wants me to sit in a draft. *(Working around the table, counting places)* It would be hard enough to play bridge on this thing. Imagine a whole family eating breakfast here.

MRS. PARKER. Perhaps it's just for us.

MR. PARKER. *(Roaring and crossing down* C.*)* What's the matter? Aren't we good enough to eat with the rest of them?

MRS. PARKER. *(Rising and crossing to him)* James, dear, control yourself. Just because the grandmother is a wee bit eccentric—

MR. PARKER. Sending someone a pogo stick covered with ice cream—

MRS. PARKER. Whipped cream, dear.

MR. PARKER. I'll bet there was arsenic sprinkled in the whipped cream.

MRS. PARKER. Oh, dear, insanity—er—eccentricity—er—runs in a family, they say.

MR. PARKER. *(Crossing to sofa)* Bootleggers! That's probably why the old girl doesn't want to merge. She's afraid I'll uncover their illegal activities. They must have made their money somehow. *(Sitting)* He's never at the office. He'd rather stay home and take the engine out of the automobile.

MRS. PARKER. *(With a look upstage, crossing to him)* Darling, don't lose your temper. You said you *needed* to merge with his company.

MR. PARKER. I do! He's got that government contract.

MRS. PARKER. Are you sure he has? Do you *know?*

MR. PARKER. I wouldn't stay here another minute if I didn't.

MRS. PARKER. Well, then, we've got to make the best of it. *(Confidently sitting beside him)* Aren't we silly? Just because that peculiar girl said those things we feel like throwing everything over.

MR. PARKER. That peculiar girl happens to be a relative. For all we know they may be all nuts back in St. Peter's.

MRS. PARKER. Oh, I'm sure they're not nuts.

REGINALD. *(Enters from up L. singing "Heigh-ho —heigh-ho." He is in his coveralls and carrying a hammer)* Morning, folks! *(Trips down step, throwing hammer in air, barely catching it. Looks at them as he crosses and hurries out the French doors.)*

MR. PARKER. *(Up and crossing C., pointing after* REGINALD *with paper)* Where's he going with that hammer?

MRS. PARKER. *(Weakly)* Probably just to hammer something.

MR. PARKER. *(Crossing to her)* How do we know it isn't *(Pauses; looks out French doors) someone?*

MRS. PARKER. James, stop thinking such things! I've been here two weeks and they've all been just lovely.

MR. PARKER. Lucid intervals, no doubt.

PENELOPE. *(Enters down the stairs; makes a dash for the piano)* Morning!

MR. *and* MRS. PARKER. Hello, Penelope!

MR. PARKER. *(As* PENELOPE *bangs away)* You can't tell me there's not something wrong with that child.

MRS. PARKER. She just loves music.

MR. PARKER. Then why does she play the piano?!

MRS. PARKER. *(To* PENELOPE*)* Won't you be late for school, Penelope?

PENELOPE. *(Busy with her scales)* What?

MRS. PARKER. I said—won't you be late for school?

PENELOPE. I'm not going.

MR. PARKER. *(Giving up)* And that's that! *(Slams paper on table)* She's not going. I suppose she'll be here all day loving her music. What a way to bring up a child!

MRS. PARKER. *(Concerned)* James, perhaps you need another pill.

MR. PARKER. I had a pill. *(With a look toward* PENELOPE*)* I'm still seeing things.

LAURA. *(Entering from up L., determinedly cheerful and gay)* Good morning, everyone! *(To* PENELOPE*)* Not today, darling. Mother has a headache. *(Beaming)* And how are the Parkers this glorious day?

MRS. PARKER. I'm splendid, thank you.

ESSIE. *(Enters up L. In the doorway)* Well, it's ready. Shall I bring it in?

LAURA. Yes, Essie. You may serve breakfast. (ESSIE *exits up L. Crossing to study door)* Some of us have eaten but I thought it would be nice to set this table in here, overlooking the garden. *(At study door)* Warry, breakfast is ready. *(Turning and crossing to below breakfast table)* Penelope, see if Marcia is in the garden, will you? (PENELOPE *goes outside. As* PENELOPE *exits,* LAURA *goes up to piano bench.)*

WARRY. *(Coming out of the study with* LILY*)* Good morning, Mother.

LAURA. *(Sliding the piano bench to the upstage end of table)* Morning, dear. Will you bring another chair over to the table, please? *(Glaring at* LILY*)* Oh—hello!

LILY. *(Warmly)* Hello, Laura!

(WARRY *is bringing the extra chair over to the table as* PENELOPE *enters with* SHERWIN *and* MARCIA, *who is carrying small bouquet of flowers.)*

MARCIA. Good morning!

(EVERYONE *speaks to* MARCIA.)

ACT III   EVERY FAMILY HAS ONE   89

PENELOPE. *(Sitting at the table on the piano bench)* Pops said he'd be in for a cup of coffee.

LAURA. Sit down, everyone, sit down—

(In the general movement, LILY crosses and sits in chair down L. of table; WARRY sits up L. of table by LILY; MRS. PARKER crosses below table to easy chair; MR. PARKER crosses above table to chair up R. of table.)

MR. PARKER. *(Going to the table; sitting uncomfortably)* Didn't you go to a lot of bother to eat in here?

LAURA. We often do. I get so sick of the dining room.

(MR. PARKER *looks at her sharply.)*

MRS. PARKER. *(Sitting in easy chair next to MR. PARKER, SHERWIN holding chair for her)* I—I think it's a charming idea. The garden is so lovely.

MR. PARKER. *(As ESSIE enters carrying a tray)* It's damp!

LAURA. Marcia, do you want something to eat?

MARCIA. *(Crossing to upstage end of table, above sofa, to fix flowers)* No, thanks, Mother. I had some coffee a little while ago.

(LAURA *indicates that* SHERWIN *is to sit on ottoman below table.* ESSIE *first puts plate of toast down beside* LAURA'S *place, then serves* PENELOPE.)

PENELOPE. *(As* ESSIE *serves her)* Oatmeal? Good night, it isn't winter!

(ESSIE *puts butter over between* PENELOPE *and* LAURA, *and marmalade directly in front of* PENELOPE.)

ESSIE. No, but we had some left from *last* winter and your mother said to use it.

MR. PARKER. Why aren't you in school today, Penelope?

(As ESSIE *"looks over" the table for anything forgotten.)*

LAURA. *(Standing at her place before the piano bench beside* PENELOPE*)* Yes, Penelope, why aren't you?

PENELOPE. *(Simply)* Because it's Saturday.

LAURA. Goodness, yes—so it is. *(Sits by* PENELOPE. ESSIE *goes out up* L. *Pause while* EVERYONE *eats)* Penelope, pass Mrs. Parker the marmalade.

(PENELOPE *holds marmalade dish up toward* MRS. PARKER *conspicuously.)*

MRS. PARKER. I much prefer just a pat of butter

LAURA. But you must try the marmalade. I made it —out of carrots.

MRS. PARKER. I'm sure it's delicious but I'd rather have just a pat—

MR. PARKER. *(To* PENELOPE, *who then puts down marmalade)* You ought to eat that cereal. Think of all the little girls who wish they could have nice warm cereal with cream.

PENELOPE. *(Thrusting it under his nose)* They can have my share any time. *(Putting oatmeal back on her plate as he pushes it away.)*

(During silence while ALL *eat as* ESSIE *enters with the coffee percolator.)*

ESSIE. *(Turns to* MARCIA *after putting the percolator on the table by* LAURA*)* You ought to eat some-

thing, Miss Marcia. You're thin as a rail. You know what happened to my sister, Sadie.
LAURA. A tragedy, Essie—but don't talk about it now.
ESSIE. *(In arch up* C.*)* Sadie was nearly a bride, too. (ESSIE *starts out, then sadly, poking head into room over* L. *bookcase)* She never got to the altar. *(She exits.)*

(As ESSIE *exits,* MARCIA *comes around downstage end of sofa and sits on arm. After finishing arranging the flowers in vase on table.)*

MR. PARKER. *(Exasperated)* Bessie, I'm crowded enough without you banging me with your elbows.
MRS. PARKER. I'm just trying to reach the butter.
LAURA. *Do* try the marmalade, Mrs. Parker. (PENELOPE *same business with marmalade)* I made it out of carrots.
REGINALD. *(As he enters by French doors)* Well, how's the family feel this morning?

(PENELOPE *puts down marmalade.)*

LAURA. Reginald, those overalls! Do you want some breakfast?
REGINALD. I had a stack of wheat cakes out in the kitchen. But I will have a cup of coffee. *(Crossing above table to* LAURA'S L.*)*
LAURA. *(Pouring the coffee)* Penelope, you still haven't passed Mrs. Parker the marmalade.

(PENELOPE *passes the marmalade and* MR. PARKER *passes it to* MRS. PARKER.*)*

MRS. PARKER. All I want is just a pat of—
LAURA. Here's your coffee, Reginald.

REGINALD. Thanks, Laura. *(He takes his coffee and sits next to* MARCIA *on the couch.)*

MR. PARKER. *(To* LILY*)* How do you feel this morning, Miss Reardon?

LILY. Oh, just perfectly wonderful, thank you.

LAURA. Lily, you and Warry must go off on a *long* hike somewhere today.

WARRY. That's a swell idea!

MR. PARKER. Did you sleep well, Miss Reardon?

LILY. Yes, but I had to count relatives.

MR. PARKER. Count relatives?

LILY. Counting *my* relatives is much more fun than counting sheep.

MR. PARKER. *(Interested)* You must have a lot of relatives.

LILY. Indeed I have. I guess we've got a little of everything. We even have an uncle who plays the trombone—on street corners.

LAURA. *(Anxiously)* Warry, why don't you and Lily start *now?*

WARRY. Wait until we finish our breakfast.

NANA. *(Entering from up* L.*)* What is this? The living room looks like a cafeteria. *(Crossing down to* REGINALD*)* I see you're all dolled up to do more wreckage, Reginald.

REGINALD. Always belittlin', Nana. *(Putting his cup and saucer back on table as* NANA *goes behind table)* A man's home is no longer his castle.

MRS. PARKER. Do you think someone could possibly pass me the butter?

(No one pays any attention.)

MR. PARKER. *(To* LILY*)* I'm thinking of visiting St. Peter's next summer.

LILY. You must stay with us.

MR. PARKER. Thank you. Aren't you kind?

ACT III EVERY FAMILY HAS ONE 93

LILY. Not at all. We take in tourists every summer. But we'll give *you* a rate.

PENELOPE. *(Suddenly, pointing at* WARRY*)* Look, Moms, Warry shaved today— Warry shaved today! He's all cut.

WARRY. I shave every day. *(Turning to* LILY*)* When we go on our hike I'll read some of my book to you. You know, you've given me some ideas for a new one. I'm going to write about a girl like you, a child of tragedy. Oh, not that any of us here hold it against *you*.

MR. PARKER. *(Quickly)* What kind of tragedy?

LAURA. *(Loudly)* Mrs. Parker, do you like my marmalade?

LILY. *(Rising and crossing near* C.*)* Laura, you hold it against me. I can tell you do. Oh, I should never have come. *(Tearfully)* Why did you invite me? Did you want to *(Sticking pin business)* stick pins in me? It's not my fault. I can't stand any more. *(She runs out through the French doors.)*

WARRY. *(Rising and running to French doors)* Lily, come back! Lily! *(Turning to* LAURA*)* Mother, if that girl does something desperate it's *your* fault. *(He runs out after her.)*

LAURA. *(Limply)* My fault? *(Rises.)*

MR. PARKER. Why does he call her a *child of tragedy?*

LAURA. *(Passing one piece of toast after another directly to him.* MR. PARKER *rises halfway out of his chair as the toast piles up in his hands)* Do have some more toast, Mr. Parker. We—we were going to have doughnuts but they just got up and walked away.

MRS. PARKER. Walked away?

LAURA. Somebody ate them. *(Sits.)*

MR. PARKER. *(As he dumps toast back onto plate)* Well, why didn't you say so? *(Sits.)*

PENELOPE. *Pops* ate 'em.

MRS. PARKER. I wish someone would pass me the butter.

MR. PARKER. I wish you'd stop poking me in the ribs, Bessie.

MRS. PARKER. You're practically sitting on top of me. *(As she turns chair slightly downstage)* Move away a bit.

MR. PARKER. If I move one inch I'll be out in the garden. And stop asking for the butter.

SHERWIN. *(Shocked)* Father, don't raise your voice like that.

MR. PARKER. I've had enough to raise my voice about.

LAURA. *(Passing the butter to* MRS. PARKER*)* Really, Mrs. Parker, why didn't you ask for the butter?

MRS. PARKER. *(Hurt)* I'm sorry if you all object to my using a little butter on my toast. I might expect it from Mrs. Reardon but when my own husband screams at me. *(She reaches for her handkerchief.)*

MR. PARKER. Bessie, stop sniveling. You remind me of your mother.

MRS. PARKER. What was wrong with my mother?!

MR. PARKER. Don't tempt me— *(Inhales very audibly)* or I'll tell you.

NANA. *(Crossing to above end of table and rubbing her hands with glee)* Ah, the showdown!

MRS. PARKER. *(Tearfully)* You—you dare to talk about my mother?

MR. PARKER. *(Getting up at the table and crossing down R.)* I'll even talk about your brother Wilbur.

MRS. PARKER. You leave Wilbur out of this! What about *your* brother Clarence?

MR. PARKER. Clarence was just unfortunate in his companions.

MRS. PARKER. Demon rum was his only companion.

MR. PARKER. You talk about rum—*you* with that *(Pause; audibly inhales)* Aunt Fanny of yours!

SHERWIN. *(Rising and going between them)* Father—Mother, please! I've never heard you like this.

ESSIE. *(Entering from up L. with the morning mail)* If you ask me it looks like the first of the month, all this mail that come. *(Handing the mail to* NANA*)* Of course nobody asked me.

NANA. *(Taking the mail)* That's right, Essie. Nobody asked you. (NANA *goes above table to get letter opener.)*

(ESSIE *exits up* L.)

MRS. PARKER. *(Rising)* I hope everybody noticed I didn't touch the butter.

LAURA. *(Furiously)* Will you shut up about the butter?! *(Rising and thrusting butter at her as* NANA *comes to* L.C. *From behind table* L.C.*)* Take all the butter. Who cares?

MRS. PARKER. *(Turning on* LAURA*)* How dare you tell me to shut up?!

NANA. *(With boxing pose, loudly)* Paging Joe Louis! Paging Joe Louis!

LAURA. *(Reacting to* REGINALD *and pushing in* WARRY'S *chair. Unhappily)* Accusing me of hoarding butter!

MRS. PARKER. And furthermore I think your marmalade is terrible!

LAURA. How dare you insult my marmalade?

NANA. *(Over a letter, turning toward him)* Reginald, here is very bad news. Very bad indeed.

REGINALD. *(Up and going to her)* What is it, Mother?

NANA. About that government contract. *(Shaking her head)* It's all off. Oh, and we were counting on it so.

REGINALD. *(Crossing up L., taking letter, but no chance to look at it)* Say, that is a blow.

LAURA. *(Going to NANA)* That wonderful government deal has fallen through? (NANA *nods*) Oh, I just can't stand any more! *(Sits in chair down L. of table.)*

MR. PARKER. Neither can we. *(Crosses to C. and turns)* Come along, Bessie. (MRS. PARKER *goes above table and out upstairs*) I've had fifty-four years of breakfasts. But never a breakfast like this. *(Angrily)* Sherwin, excuse yourself. We have some packing to do.

SHERWIN. Excuse me, please. *(Exits upstairs.)*

MR. PARKER. *(Sneezes loudly)* You and your garden! *(Exits upstairs.)*

REGINALD. *(Now looking at letter; crosses around to below sofa)* But this—this is a clothing advertisement.

NANA. Of course it is. I just wanted to lay it on thick. And I did. *(Triumphantly)* Hurray, we're rid of the Parkers!

LAURA. Gracious, do you think that government contract had anything to do with—?

NANA. Certainly I do. Don't you?

PENELOPE. *(Alone at the table)* Do I really have to eat this oatmeal?

LAURA. *(Preoccupied)* No, go outside and play, Penelope. *(With amazing speed PENELOPE jumps up from the table and dashes out through the French doors yelling: "Oh, Maudie!")* That must be why he wanted to merge with Reginald. He knew about the contract. *(Rises)* I did mention it to Mrs. Parker (NANA *reacts to* REGINALD) but she promised not to tell him. *(Tearfully)* Oh, dear, I wanted my baby to marry into the Four Hundred.

NANA. If that Mrs. Parker belongs to the Four Hundred she's one of the zeros.

LAURA. *(Hurries to the study)* I feel like going off somewhere—and dying.

REGINALD. *(Going after her)* Now, Laura, he'd have found out about the contract anyway. It isn't your fault. *(Exits.)*

MARCIA. *(Relieved, stands)* Well, it seems no society for baby. Thank my lucky star.

NANA. Thank *me*.

MARCIA. Yes, I have suspected my darling grandmother of doing some arranging. *(Going to her)* Did you bring little Lily here?

NANA. No, but I did ask little Lily to spill some beans.

MARCIA. And what beans! Are those things true?

NANA. St. Peter's is a one-horse town, Marcia. And most of our relatives are plain people. But, so help me, none of them are counterfeiters.

MARCIA. And Mother talked about the Galloways! *(Suddenly)* I'm going to telephone Todd.

NANA. *(As MARCIA goes to the phone)* Stop! He's not there.

MARCIA. He—he hasn't gone away?

NANA. Yes, but he'll be back tonight.

MARCIA. Nana, have you done some more arranging?

NANA. You'll find out at the proper time.

MARCIA. *(Kissing her)* You're my favorite grandmother!

NANA. *(Crossing to below table and pushing in chair)* Get away! I hate sentimentality.

LAURA. *(Coming in from the study, followed by* REGINALD*)* Oh, what will I tell everyone? We're ruined, disgraced, mutilated beyond recognition. Or do I mean humiliated?

REGINALD. Laura, we're well rid of those people. Aren't you glad you found out about them before Marcia married Sherwin?

LAURA. *(Sitting on the sofa)* Oh, go outside and tinker! Leave me with my grief.

REGINALD. *(Helplessly)* Mother, see what you can do with her. *(Goes out through French doors.)*

MARCIA. *(Going to* LAURA*)* Mother, don't feel so bad about this. *(Sits)* I don't.

LAURA. But my dear, all the invitations are out. And the presents are just pouring in. We've got to have a wedding.

MARCIA. *(Looking at* NANA *and winking)* Very well, I'll look around and see what I can do.

LAURA. Darling, will you? Somebody in town here —*without any family!*

NANA. I hope you've learned your lesson, Laura. Being ashamed of your own relatives, putting on airs, you had this coming to you.

LAURA. *(Meekly)* I know I did.

NANA. Then it's all been worthwhile *(Sits below table on chair* R. *of ottoman.)*

ESSIE. *(Enters up* L. *to the doorway up* C.*)* What are we having for lunch?

LAURA. Lunch? Lunch? We're not going to have any lunch—ever.

ESSIE. Can't make me mad. *(Curiously)* Are the Parkers going some place? They're tearing down the stairs carrying their suitcases.

LAURA. *(Sternly)* Essie, you must have lots to do in the kitchen. (ESSIE *exits up* L. *Rising and crossing down* L.*)* Do you suppose those dreadful people are leaving without thanking their hostess?

MR. PARKER. *(Entering downstairs with* MRS. PARKER *and* SHERWIN, *all dressed for leaving,* MR. PARKER *and* SHERWIN *carrying suitcases)* Mrs. Reardon, I'm sure you understand.

(MRS. PARKER *stands by* L. *of arch,* MR. PARKER *at* C., SHERWIN *at* R.*)*

ACT III   EVERY FAMILY HAS ONE   99

LAURA. Understand what?
MR. PARKER. We feel it necessary to postpone the wedding—
LAURA. *(Stiffly)* Wedding? Wedding? Oh, the wedding—
MRS. PARKER. We're all quite upset.
NANA. So are we. That's why we've decided we can't let Marcia marry Sherwin.
MR. PARKER. *(Enraged—one step down stage)* You—you not allow?
MRS. PARKER. *(Steps down from platform to step)* Outrageous!
NANA. *(Smugly)* We believe in heredity. And you know his Uncle Clarence.
LAURA. Don't forget *(Putting her arm around* MARCIA's *shoulder)* his Aunt Fanny!
MR. PARKER. Are you insinuating, madam, that my family isn't good enough—
NANA. I wasn't insinuating, sir. I was *telling* you.
MRS. PARKER. Come, James. *(He starts cross up toward steps)* Don't bother with these—these *immigrants!* *(To C. of archway.)*
MR. PARKER. *(In the archway at L.)* I'll also have you understand this was the first time there ever was a harsh word between Bessie and me. It must be the environment. Goodbye. *(Starts out up R.)*
MRS. PARKER. Come, Sherwin! *(As she goes out up R.)*
SHERWIN. I'm—I'm sorry, Marcia, but Mother and Father seem quite determined.
MARCIA. *(Quietly)* That's all right, Sherwin. It isn't your fault.
MRS. PARKER. *(Off)* Sherwin!
SHERWIN. Coming, Mother! *(Follows his parents out up R.)*
LAURA. *(Pacing up and down)* Immigrants? Did she mean *us?* Oh, the nerve! The colossal nerve! *(To* NANA*)* Why didn't somebody say something?

NANA. *(Chuckling)* I was too busy laughing.
LAURA. I didn't see anything funny.
NANA. I did. Bessie's slip was hanging six inches.
MARCIA. *(With a contented sigh, sitting on upstage end of sofa)* Well, I guess the excitement is over. The Parkers have gone.

(There is a tremendous CRASH from offstage. ALL rush to the French doors. REGINALD enters from the French doors, pale and shaken. He sinks down on ottoman.)

LAURA. Reginald, what was that explosion?
REGINALD. The brake. I forgot to adjust the brake. And the car—the car rolled down the driveway.
NANA. I knew that would happen eventually. Is the car ruined?
REGINALD. *(Crossing above table to* C.*)* No, but you should see the Parkers' roadster. (MARCIA, *who didn't get a good look out window before, now down to look out)* Our car smacked right into it!
LAURA. *(Happily, crossing to him)* You darling, you did it on purpose!
NANA. They're the kind of people who sue. *(Sitting on downstage end of sofa.)*
LAURA. It's a private driveway. They had no right to park their car in it. *(Solicitously)* Reginald, you look faint. *(Taking him up* C.*)* Come upstairs and rest a bit.
REGINALD. *(Rising)* Guess maybe I'd better.
LAURA. *(Helping him up onto steps)* I'm only sorry about one thing, dear. That you didn't wait.
REGINALD. Wait for what?
LAURA. Wait until the Parkers were *in* their car.
REGINALD. I did.

(LAURA *and* REGINALD *go upstairs.)*

NANA. *(Proudly.* MARCIA *sits chair below table* R., *laughing)* That's my son!

(WARRY *and* LILY *enter through the French doors.)*

NANA. Well, the Parkers are gone. You acted your part nobly.
LILY. *(Crossing to* C.) I thought I did pretty well for such short notice.
NANA. Of course, you did overdo it a bit. I mean, nobody could believe that *I* was whacky, but thank you, anyway.
LILY. *(Rest of way to her)* Don't thank me. I enjoyed it.
WARRY. *(Crossing to* LILY) What are you two talking about?
LILY. Most of the things I've said here were exaggerations.
WARRY. You're—you're not Lily's daughter?
LILY. Oh, I'm Lily's daughter—but a different Lily. The other Lily moved to Buffalo. My mother does needlework and Father works in a bank.
WARRY. *(Hurt)* Then you're not a child of tragedy?
LILY. Well, I had to wear a brace on my teeth and—
WARRY. What a rotten trick to play on anyone! And I believed you. I trusted you. And all the time your parents are perfectly respectable. *(Disgustedly. Over to column up* R.C.; *leans head against arm)* This time I *am* through with women!
LILY. Warry, it's not my fault my parents are respectable.
WARRY. How could you deceive me? You haven't suffered at all.
LILY. *(Going to him)* I suffered in love.
WARRY. *Anyone* can suffer in love.
NANA. *(Winking at* LILY) No one can suffer like

Lily suffered. Lily, child, tell Warry how that brute tortured you. It makes my blood boil. Oh, the things he did!

WARRY. *(Interested—down to above chair R.C.)* Did he really?

LILY. *(Dramatically—down to NANA)* Warry, don't force me to remember. That part of my life is a closed chapter. *Please* don't make me tell you.

ESSIE. *(Entering up L.)* Special delivery for Mr. Warry! *(She hands him the letter.)*

WARRY. *(Looking at it)* Why, it's from the publishers!

MARCIA. *(Stands)* Oh, hurry, Warry—open it!

WARRY. I can't. *(Drops letter)* I'm weak. *(Sinks on ottoman)* Oh, but they don't send rejection slips special delivery, do they? *(Finally retrieves it after fumbling—tears the letter open.)*

ESSIE. *(Watching him read the letter)* I wrote a story for *True Confessions* once. They sent it back. *(Sadly.)*

NANA. *(Watching WARRY)* Oh, Essie—hush!

WARRY. *(Overjoyed)* Nana, they like the book! (LILY *down to him. His face falls)* But—but they don't understand it. *(Stands and crosses to* NANA. LILY *gives R.)* Nana, they think it's—it's *funny!*

NANA. *(Rises)* What do you care as long as they publish it?

WARRY. *(Reading)* "In these times it is important to laugh and your satire is one of the funniest to come to our attention. We also think Aggie and John are the most comical lovers since—" Oh, I can't say it. How could they be so stupid? *(Sits down on upstage end of sofa, face buried in his hands.)*

NANA. *(Taking the letter and reading as she goes to down L. end of sofa)* "The most comical lovers since Mickey and Minnie Mouse."

ESSIE. Oh, I just love Minnie Mouse. *(Excitedly)*

Maybe they'll make one of them animated cartoons out of Mr. Warry's book.
WARRY. *(With dignity)* Essie, go do the laundry.
ESSIE. This ain't Monday.
NANA. *(Crossing above sofa to* ESSIE*)* Go do the laundry, anyway.

(ESSIE *shakes her head bewilderedly and exits up* L.*)*

WARRY. *(A beaten figure—rises)* I think this is the end of the world for me. *(Going to the study door)* I'm going to be in here *hiding* for the rest of the day. Tomorrow I shall probably join a monastery. *(Shuddering)* "Minnie Mouse"—*my* Aggie! *(He goes into the study.)*
LILY. *(Crossing to down* L.*)* Oh, poor Warry!
MARCIA. They're going to publish his book. *(Sits)* That's all that matters.
NANA. Come to think of it, that book *was* funny!
LILY. And I had to go disappoint him, too. I've broken his heart.
NANA. *(Drops down to* LILY*)* Go on in and mend it.
LILY. But he said not to disturb him.
NANA. He didn't mean you.
LILY. *(Goes to study door)* Then if you'll excuse me I have some mending to do. *(Smiling at them)* This is much better than a stock company. *(She goes into the study.)*
LAURA. *(Entering from up* L.*)* Where's Warry? Essie just told me they're making a movie out of that lovely book of his. My baby, a genius!
NANA. They're *publishing* his book. But leave him alone right now. He wrote a tragedy and they're publishing it as a comedy. His heart is broken.
LAURA. Isn't he ungrateful! When I read his book I couldn't laugh or cry. I just felt *numb*. *(To* MARCIA—*crossing to her)* Darling, hadn't you better get

on the telephone and call up all those nice young men you know and tell them the wedding is off?
　MARCIA. I've got the nice young man, Mother.
　LAURA. So soon? Who is it, darling?
　MARCIA. *(Defensively and turning)* It's Todd Galloway.
　LAURA. *(Happily)* Todd? Oh, I've always liked him so much.
　NANA. *(Gasping)* What was that?
　LAURA. And he has no family to brag about, thank heaven!
　MARCIA. And we love each other very much.
　LAURA. *(Puts arm around* MARCIA*)* I always think it's so nice to marry someone you love.
　MARCIA. Then you're not going to be difficult about it?
　LAURA. Difficult! *Me?* When was I ever difficult about anything? (MARCIA *and* NANA *sink on chair and sofa.)*　　　　　　　　　　*(WARN Curtain.)*
　PENELOPE. *(Skips in through the French doors)* Well, Nana, I saw them go! Where's my dollar?
　LAURA. What dollar?
　PENELOPE. Nana promised me a dollar if I'd practice my piano all the time while Mrs. Parker was here.
　NANA. *(Fishing in her pocket)* Here, you highway woman! *(Hands her the dollar.)*
　PFNELOPE. What? No tax? (NANA *hits her on behind as* PENELOPE *goes down and around table behind sofa.)*
　LAURA. Nana, you should be ashamed. But I wish I'd thought of it first.
　ESSIE. *(Entering from up* L. *with a telegram)* Special delivery letters and telegrams— My, what a day!
　LAURA. *(As* LAURA *crosses up* C. ESSIE *hands her the telegram)* For me?
　FSSIE. Says "Laura Reardon" on it.

ACT III   EVERY FAMILY HAS ONE   105

(As ESSIE *exits,* WARRY *and* LILY *enter from study.*

LAURA. But I hate these things. —More than ever now. *(Opens it)* It's from Buffalo. (NANA *reacts.* PENELOPE *crosses to* LAURA'S L. *to read telegram with her. Reading it)* "Saw announcement of Marcia's wedding in papers, and am coming to visit you. Will arrive shortly. It's been years. Lily." *(Puzzled)* Lily—in Buffalo. What Lily can that be? *(Thinking —crossing down to* NANA. PENELOPE *gives* R. *to above bench)* Why, it must be that Lily who did the lovely needlework. Reverend Perkins' daughter. The one who had the case on Cousin Susie's son, Harry. *(Delightedly, turning to* MARCIA*)* Oh, it will be just lovely having *her* here!

LILY. *(Crossing to* LAURA*)* But Laura, you're all wrong. That's my mother you're talking about.

LAURA. Your mother? *Your* mother?? Then what Lily is this?

NANA. That's *the* Lily.

LAURA. The Lily!!! *(As she sinks onto ottoman down* L. *of table)* Oh! *(Groans as* PENELOPE *grabs glass of water from table, thrusting it at* LAURA *as)*

THE CURTAIN FALLS VERY QUICKLY

EVERY FAMILY HAS ONE

SOUND CUES

Act I

Typing
>Warning: LAURA. —And leave that slingshot here! I'm sure Maudie hasn't a slingshot.
>Cue: LAURA. —Of course, *I* have to make concessions but then that's why mothers are born.

(Sudden sound of someone typing furiously on an old and noisy typewriter L. from study) Continues until

>Cue: marry into a family as fine as our own.

Clock Striking
>Warning: MRS. PARKER. —Never a harsh word, never a quarrel.
>Cue: MRS. PARKER. —But, remember, spare the rod and—
>>(Chimes 5)

Hammering
>Warning: LAURA. —The Parkers will be here any minute now.
>Cue: NANA. Don't I know it?
>>(Loud hammering on metal from driveway R. REGINALD working on car. Continues until Cue: Reginald, you come in here this very minute.)

SOUND CUES

Hammering
>Warning: LAURA. —none of them would come —thank goodness.
>CUE: LAURA. —I'm going to ask that fortune-teller in Newark.
>(More hammering from driveway. Continues until "some quiet hobby like stamps or guppies.")

Typing
>Warning: LAURA. —it was none of our business whom she married as long as she keeps him up there.
>CUE: LAURA. —like stamps or guppies.
>(Typing begins as hammering stops. Continues through CUE, Maybe he's a genius.)

Typing
>Warning: NANA. —I'm going to put on my comfortable shoes.
>CUE: MARCIA. —Oh, Warry, you haven't seen my dress. (Stops on "Let me finish this sentence.")

ACT II

Music (for radio on stage)
>*Begin* as Curtain rises.
>*End:* LAURA. —Oh, dear, and I haven't even an aspirin in the house.
>(Turns off radio.)

Glass Crash
>Warning: MRS. PARKER. —Whipped cream, dear. How very peculiar.
>CUE: MR. PARKER. —Yes, ha! ha!
>(All laugh uncomfortably. Sudden crash of glass R. outside French doors.)

Act III

Car Crash
Warning: LAURA. —I know I did.
CUE: MARCIA. —Well, I guess the excitement is over. The Parkers have gone.
　(Tremendous crash at R. outside French doors.)

EVERY FAMILY HAS ONE

DECORATIVE PROPERTIES

1. Four large pictures.
2. Two small pictures.
3. Glass curtains on French windows.
4. Drapes on hall windows.
5. Runner on gate leg table.
6. Vase of flowers on davenport table.
7. Two bowls of flowers, one on each bookcase.
8. Books and book ends on gate leg table.
9. Books in bookcases.
10. Bric-a-brac in bookcases.
11. Cigarette case on gate leg table.
12. Two hanging ivy bowls with ivy in French window.

SET PROPERTIES

ACT ONE AND TWO

1. Piano and bench up R.
2. Drop leaf, gate leg table R.
3. Easy chair R. of table.
4. Ottoman L. of table.
5. Small footstool at easy chair.
6. Sofa L.C.
7. Davenport table behind sofa.
8. Radio-phonograph up L.

PROPERTIES

9. Straight chair near radio.
10. Floor lamp at radio.
11. Table lamp on piano.
12. Mantel clock on piano.
13. Telephone table at stairway.
14. Telephone on table.
15. Four sofa cushions. Two on sofa. Two on window seat.
16. Ashtray on davenport table.

ACT THREE—*ADD:*

1. One dining room chair.

SET PROPERTIES OFF STAGE

1. Two dining room chairs off L. Brought in during Act 3.

HAND PROPERTIES

ACT ONE

1. Two flower bowls with flowers, L., LAURA.
2. Sheet music and scale exercise books, on piano, PENELOPE.
3. Slingshot, on piano, PENELOPE.
4. Bing Crosby album of records, R., NANA.
5. Box of chocolate mints, R., NANA.
6. Glass of milk and four doughnuts on plate, L., ESSIE.
7. Tool kit with hammer, saw and big wrench, L., REGINALD.
8. Wedding invitations, 25, table behind sofa, LAURA.
9. Pen and ink desk set, table behind sofa, LAURA.
10. Screwdriver, L., REGINALD.

PROPERTIES

11. Cooking spoon, L., ESSIE.
12. Eyeshade, L., WARRY.
13. Pencil, L., WARRY.
14. Slip with address, L., NANA.
15. Luggage, two men's overnight bags, R., PARKERS.
16. Work basket with embroidery, in bookcase, NANA.
17. Copy of the *New Yorker*, table R.C., NANA.
18. Telegram, L., REGINALD.

ACT TWO

1. Copy of the *New Yorker*, on occasional chair, NANA.
2. Slingshot, on gate leg table, PENELOPE.
3. Luggage—overnight bag, R., LILY.

ACT THREE

1. Tablecloth, on gate leg table.
2. Napkins, eight, on gate leg table.
3. Silverware for eight, on gate leg table.
4. Plates, cups, saucers, glasses for eight (Breakfast), on gate leg table.
5. Sugar and creamer, on gate leg table.
6. Orange juice in seven glasses, on gate leg table.
7. Milk in one glass and pitcher, on gate leg table.
8. New York newspaper, on davenport table.
9. Hot pad, on gate leg table.
10. Small bouquet of flowers, R., MARCIA.
11. Coffee percolator and coffee, L., ESSIE.
12. Tray with one dish of oatmeal and plate of toast, dish of marmalade and dish of butter, L., ESSIE.
13. Letters for morning mail, L., ESSIE.
14. Letter opener, on davenport table, LAURA.
15. Dollar bill, L., NANA.
16. Letter, L., ESSIE.

17. Hammer, L., REGINALD.
18. Special delivery letter, L., ESSIE.
19. Dishcloth, L., ESSIE.
20. Luggage (two bags from Act One plus one more ladies' bag), L., PARKERS.
21. Telegram L., ESSIE.

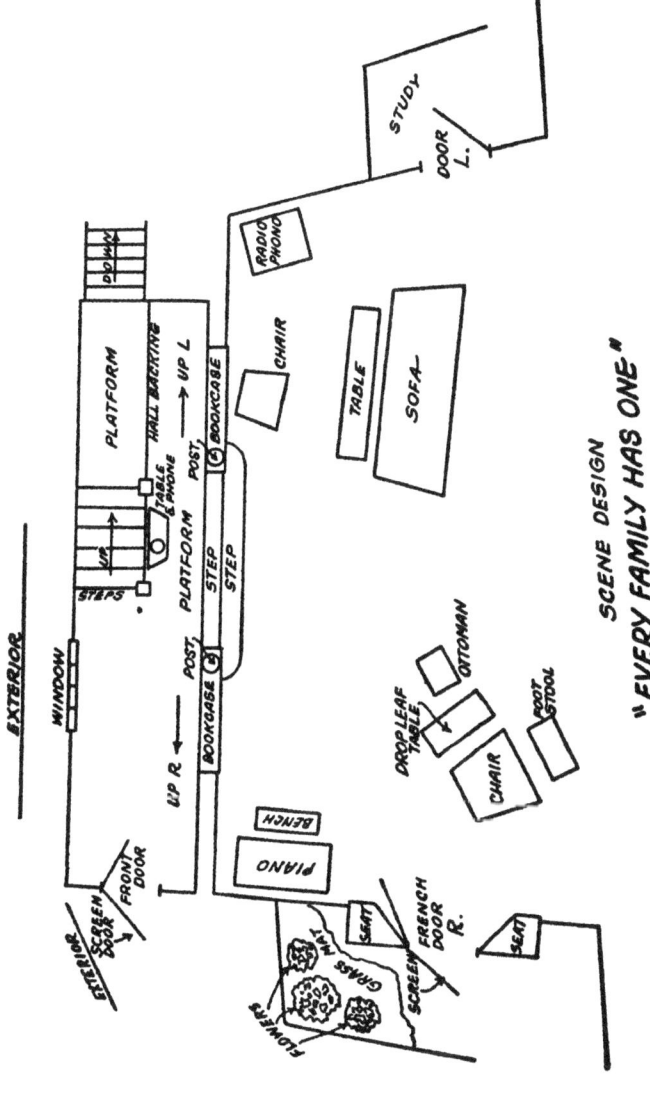

SCENE DESIGN
"EVERY FAMILY HAS ONE"

www.ingramcontent.com/pod-product-compliance
Lightning Source LLC
Chambersburg PA
CBHW070644300426
44111CB00013B/2262